A Modern Heathen's Guide to Norse Paganism:

The Earth-Centered Religion that Empowers Us to Embrace Our Inner Viking and Take Charge of Our Fate

Quinby C. Larson

Contents

Introduction

Less than a year after graduating from school I left my hometown in Washington state and moved with a friend to Alaska. We lived for six months in a hundred-year-old cabin on a gold mining claim, more than a hundred and sixty miles northeast of Fairbanks. It was late spring. We were there to "brush the lines" of a gold mining claim so that the edges of the 40-acre property were cleared and easy to identify.

Our first morning there we were jolted awake by pounding on the door. Standing just outside, with fist raised to knock again was a tall sinewy man with shaggy, grey hair and a scruffy beard. He was there to invite us to breakfast. He told us that because we were new to the area, it was okay if we showed up empty-handed, this once. He gave us directions, told us to bring our own dishes, and hurry on over. In less than a minute he was gone. We quickly dressed and headed out the door. It was six o'clock in the morning.

A dozen people were wandering in and out of an even smaller cabin, drinking coffee and visiting with neighbors when we arrived. I got out and a tired-looking woman in mukluks waved and motioned for me to come. We shared introductions as she led me over to a man barely out of his teens. He was sitting on a stump in front of an open fire. It was his breakfast I was there to consume.

The small fire pit was surrounded by softball size stones. An oven rack sat on top holding an industrial-size stockpot. Without looking up, he told me he was making "miner's breakfast."

"First, you sauté onions, peppers, and potatoes. Then you add diced chunks of whatever meat you happen to have."

"What kind is it?" I asked while peering into the large, sizzling pot, breathing in the savory, but unfamiliar aroma.

"Bear."

"Bear?" My friend, who had followed behind us, and I sputtered in unison.

The young man then proceeded to tell the story behind our breakfast. He had left the door of his cabin open to let in some sunlight and fresh air. He was relaxing on his bed, engrossed in a book when a brown bear walked in. "It had to duck its head to fit inside." He slowly grabbed his rifle that hung on the wall beside the bed. It soon became apparent that the bear was not going to leave on its own, so he had to shoot it. Then, with the help of some neighbors, he spent the night cleaning and butchering. He hadn't slept since the previous morning. Without refrigeration, the meat needed to be eaten or preserved right away.

Once the meat was cooked, he cracked a massive number of eggs into the mixture, stirring until it was all cooked through. We found out later that each of the other ingredients for the miner's breakfast was brought by someone else.

An old-timer took the time to explain to us the unwritten rules they all lived by. To be part of that community meant that you stepped up and did your part when necessary. If you need help just ask, and someone will be there for you, "but always give more help than you ask for." We were also cautioned not to commit to "what you won't follow through on."

In that environment, you had to be trustworthy, or the consequences could be severe. If others hadn't helped butcher the bear, the meat would have spoiled. Reciprocity was at the core of why that community survived through the harsh winter months. Those that helped butcher and dress out the bear now had more food for the winter.

We learned that there were some people in the greater area that wanted nothing to do with anyone else. Nothing was expected from them, but nothing was given to them either.

Years later, as I learned about Norse Paganism, I thought back on that breakfast we shared with our new community. In many ways, it was reminiscent of how the Vikings treated guests and how the guests were expected to respond. Other than the four-wheel-drive vehicles and old trucks that were parked out of the way in the dirt, that communal breakfast could have taken place a thousand years ago. The man with the bear only provided the meat but he knew that's all he needed. Some people showed up with potatoes or onions, others brought eggs or coffee. Everyone, except us newbies, knew their responsibility. Of course, there is a lot more to this religion than reciprocity and keeping your word.

The faith of my childhood told me to follow the commandments, "let God decide" and to be obedient without question. As an adult, I realized that not everything we were taught as children was always true, at least not for me.

The Abrahamic religions are filled with a doctrine that is inconsistent with reality. For example, the Bible says, "the meek shall inherit the earth" (Psalms 37:11), and "it is easier for a camel to go through the eye of a needle than for a rich man to enter the kingdom of God" (Matt. 19:24), yet we open our eyes and see the world is run, now and always has been, by the wealthy and powerful. Popular televangelists are multimillionaires.

Generation after generation has been raised to believe that men are better than women. "Men stand superior to women..." (Qur'an 4.34). Women are meant to be subservient to men, especially in marriage. "Wives, submit yourselves to your own husbands" (Ephesians 5:22). Women today, around the world, have proven that they are as intelligent, dedicated, responsible, and hard-working as men. Unfortunately, their religion has not evolved to embrace that reality.

Millions are taught "if you have faith as small as a mustard seed, you can say to this mountain, 'Move from here to there,' and it will move" (Matt. 17:20). How many have lived their entire lives under the burden of feeling that no matter how devout they are, how much they have given, and how hard they have prayed, they are still not good enough because they could not move a single hill. I've never seen a mountain move. I've studied history, in college and on my own, yet never come across a single incident in which a mountain miraculously moved. Have you? People will argue that despite the wording, it's meant symbolically. Symbolic for what? What could happen to someone or some tangible thing, that would possibly fill in for that comparison?

The only plausible answer would be that someone prayed and their loved one was healed. What does that say for all those who did the same and yet their loved ones did not recover? Science has proven that our bodies have an amazing ability to heal themselves, occasionally, and to a point.

There is evidence that prayer can sometimes help, as does meditation and positive thinking. Go into any Hindu, Buddhist, Sikh, or Jewish temple, and people have poured out their hearts there in prayer for healing, for themselves, or for someone they love. The same is true for Muslim mosques and Christian churches of every denomination. The evidence shows that there is no difference in results based on which religion you follow or what God or gods you pray to.

Many faiths, or creeds within a larger faith, have been the source of narrow-mindedness and misery in this world since the beginning of organized religion, in cultures that died away millennia ago, and it is still happening today.

God, of the Abrahamic religions, is omniscient, he knows everything, can do anything. He is also omnipresent; he sees every move of every person on earth. Every word ever uttered, or thought ever had, is known by Him. He is perfect. If something is perfect, in order to remain perfect, it must stay the same. If a change would improve it then it wasn't perfect to begin with.

Unlike monotheism, with its belief in a perfect God and unchangeable, divinely inspired scriptures, paganism adapts and changes as science, and societies advance. We become more aware. Many people, me included, had a hard time coming to terms with the idea that God was all-knowing and all-powerful, and yet he allowed so many bad things to happen in the world. Things that a perfect God could easily prevent or at least make better. The only solace for believers is "have faith, only God knows the reason why."

Pagans don't have that disconnect between what gods can do and what they actually do in the world. The gods aren't perfect, the world can be cruel and harsh. We can learn from the stories of the gods, but we don't look to them to "fix it." Instead, we look to them for strength and wisdom so that we can fix things ourselves.

Norse paganism is based on the beliefs and world views of those we call the Vikings. I would be the last to claim that they did not perpetuate misery on their victims. It was a brutal time when often physical strength determined the victor. Christianity and Islam were also violent against others at that time. Instead of judging any religious tradition, based on how people lived it a thousand years ago, it is far more important to look at how they live it today.

My name is Quinby C. Larson. I was born and raised in the Pacific Northwest, forced to follow practices of a religion I did not believe in, and never felt attached to. Those feelings of emptiness led me to learn about different religions from around the world. I studied the Western Monotheistic faiths, Judaism, Islam, and multiple Christian denominations. Not finding what I was looking for, I investigated many Eastern religions such as Buddhism, Taoism, Hinduism, and Shinto, only to circle back to the West. I began to explore older religious traditions that predated the spread of Christianity.

Ultimately, I found a faith that truly values me and every part of nature that I deeply care about. I am writing this book to empower others and educate people who want to learn more about the Old Norse's paganism, Forn Siðr, to the people who lived it in the distant past.

At face value, the violence and large-scale thievery the Vikings were known for, hardly seems like a positive, life-affirming religion. But the more I learned about the standing and rights of women, within that society, my heart and mind began to open. Being meek and humble is not my style. I'm a strong, type-A person who knows what I want in life and is willing to put the work and effort into making it happen. For me, following this path is how I remain true to myself.

Norse paganism is a belief system followed by people beginning in ancient times, which focuses on taking control of your life and valuing intelligence and action over blind obedience. Meek and subservient behavior is not practiced nor preached to men or women. On the contrary, confidence and bravery are highly rewarded and encouraged. That's good because turning the other cheek does not just seem dumb to me, it feels wrong.

I also connected with this religion because of its animistic ideology, the idea that there is a spirit in all things, not just human beings. I admire the devotion Norse Pagans have for their families, community, ancestors, animals, and the physical world. I appreciate their respect for all living things. Norse paganism is an earth-centered belief. It acknowledges that we are part of the world and need to work in and with it so that all aspects of it, including us, thrive. Ultimately, being a Norse pagan-embracing heathen rings true to me. Within this belief system, I feel validated.

Through Norse Paganism I feel empowered to stand up for what is right. That includes everything from recycling to ease the burden of landfills to standing up to racists, bigots, and bullies. It's a good thing to be determined, to speak your mind, and be honest about how you feel. Obviously, I don't encourage anyone to put themselves in harm's way, but there are always ways to help de-escalate a situation. I could go on and on about this subject, but I think you get the idea.

Today many people assume Norse paganism is a religion that supports white supremacy. It would be dishonest to say that those factions do not exist. They have used a misinterpretation of ancient text to justify their racist beliefs. It is an issue I strongly disagree with, and I address it head-on in this book.

To call Norse paganism a religion can be a bit misleading. It is not just a set of beliefs and stories. It was a way of life for the Old Norse people and is for those who follow its traditions now.

Perhaps you are struggling, questioning the validity of your beliefs. Maybe you are still going along, pasting on a façade, but feeling your true self caged behind a veneer of incredulity. For some, you have already tossed those religious beliefs from childhood aside, but feel a void left behind. If so, you might find Norse paganism interesting, especially for those looking for a religion that matches their own intuitive ideas about how things are in the world and how they should be.

This book is not an encyclopedia of Norse mythology. Instead, I have attempted to distill the values, traits, and goals of the gods from the stories and lore in which they reside. So that as you move forward in your pagan journey you can incorporate those things more intentionally into your daily life.

As a reader, I never gave much thought to the title of books. Now, in writing one of my own, I realize the importance of a well-thought-out title. I see it as a promise to my readers of what they can expect to learn here. For that reason, although unorthodox, I want to share with you why I named this book what I did.

A Modern Heathen's Guide to Norse Paganism: means I'm going to talk about the religion from the perspective of an insider, not someone that's presenting it as an outdated religion that no one in modern times would ever think was relevant to their life. There is no "one way" to be a heathen or pagan. Science has advanced, and without written documentation from the people living at that time, much has been lost. I believe that Norse Pagan gods are as real as Hindu gods, and, yes, the Christian God. The majority of modern heathens and Norse Pagans, myself included, believe that the gods exist in the unseen world, part of the "other side" that lives all around us every day, beyond the view of mortal man. They are part of that "energy" or "higher self" or "ethereal beings" that we can tap into through meditation, prayer, and other means, to help guide us in our lives.

A quick disclaimer, this isn't a guide to all of Norse Paganism. That would take many times the number of pages written here, but I will do my best to discuss and explain those areas that are covered.

The Earth-Centered Religion that Empowers Us: It is an animistic religion. The divine is all around us, in the trees and ocean, in the animals wild and domestic. There is "spirit" in everything. Because of that belief, it is important to treat the world with respect: protect the environment, leave nature in the same or better condition than when you entered it, don't overuse resources, and value the life of all beings. This belief guides me and other pagans to treat the world with reverence and respect. It is not a religion confined to one day a week inside a building. It is a way of life.

to Embrace Our Inner Viking: Most people that were raised in a church were taught the importance of being meek and humble before God. A person should not brag or boast. Instead of going by how you feel things should be, chances are you were taught that blind obedience is better than questioning. The All-father God of Norse Pagans, Odin, is a warrior god. He promotes being the best you can possibly be in all ways. Be physically fit (as much as personal health allows), accept responsibility for your actions. Claim ownership of the decisions you make. Be a leader, in full control of your life.

and Take Charge of Our Fate: This goes hand in hand with the last one. Fate or "Wyrd" plays a major role in Norse Paganism. You cannot change the day you were born or the family you were born into. You cannot change the preordained day you will die. But you and you alone can take charge of your life between those two dates. Change its trajectory away from mediocrity. Norse Paganism acknowledges that life is not fair. Some people are born healthy into successful families that love, nurture, and support them through childhood and beyond so that they can have wonderful, successful lives. Others are born into poverty or into families that abuse or neglect them. The lack of resources, and local opportunities. Those are the parts of our "fate" that we cannot control. What we can and are expected to do is to make the most of the talents or "gifts" we are given, work hard, focusing on long-term goals instead of giving in to instant gratification. We are meant to sacrifice in order to learn and grow as people. It is human nature not to place much value on something that is free and easy to acquire. Those things that make a real difference in your life, that put you in charge, take time, patience, self-sacrifice, knowledge, and hard work. Norse Pagans know that taking charge of your fate is worth the cost.

Odin is well-known as a seeker of knowledge. He sacrificed an eye for it. He hung himself on the World Tree Yggdrasil, a sacrifice to himself, to gain knowledge about the runes. Now you are following in Odin's footsteps, sacrificing your time and money in a quest for greater knowledge. I commend you for emulating the All-Father, Odin, in your quest for a richer, fuller, more meaningful life.

After reading this book, you will have a better understanding of the values and mindset of Norse pagans. Then you can choose for yourself whether to embrace the religion as a whole or take from it the parts that align best to your true self. I hope you enjoy the book.

Regards,

Quinby

Chapter 1
Norse Paganism in the 21st Century

People might imagine that modern-day Norse Pagans are middle-aged guys that still live in their parent's basement. People who spend their days putting together elaborate Viking costumes, so they can run around on the weekends playing at warrior reenactments. The reality? Some Norse Pagans do enjoy going to reenactments, maybe once or twice a year. Most don't have all that time to "play" because they are already warriors in their everyday lives. The Old Norse learned how to live and thrive in a hostile environment. The world has become much more civilized in the last 1,000 years but with so many people, all competing for success, certain traits are still needed to come out on top.

Many religions and traditions teach us to look the other way, be passive, and never question authority. Norse paganism is not one of them. Do you want to take charge of your life, achieve more than the status quo, maybe change the world? In that case, you must think with an open mind and follow your gut. You need to do the things that are required to achieve what you want in life. That does not mean breaking the law, abusing, taking advantage of others, or acting in an unethical way. As you will come to learn, acting honorably was central to the Old Norse way of life.

Norse Paganism is as relevant and useful today as it was during the time of the Vikings. Life has gotten easier, but it is far from easy. The traits and values that this belief system encourages will help a person be more responsible, confident, and motivated to achieve whatever they desire, so long as it does not infringe on others. Hard work, dedication, and sacrifice when needed are the keys to the Norse Pagan way of life. Those traits are also key for successful men and women in the military and in almost every other career field.

We can look to many of the mottoes and slogans from different military branches for guidance on how to become a better version of ourselves. The more you learn about the values of the Old Norse, the more similarities you will see between them, and the values prized in the US military, and around the world.

The Old Norse and Military Values

Growing up in an American household, I remember the surge in patriotism that washed over the country on Veterans Day. The parades and stories on the evening news of brave soldiers who risked their lives in horrific wars. We honored those that made it home alive and paid tribute to those who lost their lives on the battlefield. The longest war in U.S. history is finally over. No matter where you fall on the political spectrum, the admiration, and respect for the men and women fighting the war were unwavering. Those in the military put their lives in danger at the forefront of battles from ancient times to modern wars.

We praise the men and women in uniform for their courage, their physical strength, and agility and for their fierceness in the face of danger. Have you noticed the disconnect? We praise our soldiers, yet the children who will become soldiers are taught in school that if they "fight back" against a bully, they are equally guilty. I am not advocating schoolyard fights, but it feels wrong to punish someone for protecting themselves. It is a skill they will need in their adult life, to stand up for themselves, yet our schools preach the opposite. This is just one example. Our society is a mass of contradictions. To experience discontent is a normal reaction to such an environment. What does all of this have to do with Norse Paganism? Far more than you might think.

Learning about their principles and goals, you will see that the militaries of different countries around the world follow similar standards. There are slogans and battle cries that directly support the Old Norse beliefs on how we should live our lives.

The mottos that all military branches use are bold statements that demonstrate the most important values of that branch. The U.S. military consisted, until recently, of the Marine Corps, Navy, Army, Air Force, and Coast Guard. In 2019 a new branch, the Space Force, was added, but it is too new to have built any mottoes or traditions. So, we will focus on the original five [1].

U.S. Marines

Some of the mottos and slogans are easily recognizable, such as "Semper Fi" short for "Semper Fidelis." It is Latin for "Always Faithful." The motto is not just a phrase to be yelled back and forth between troops. It runs through the blood of service members; it is a way of life. The people serving in the marines are fully devoted to protecting their peers and their country. Loyalty, faithfulness, and respect for one's brethren are not negotiable to a U.S. marine, nor were they in a Norse Viking's life [1][2].

To a Norse Pagan, being faithful means staying the course. They do not give up on their goals when it gets difficult. They stay faithful to their quests, their missions in life. What those are is unique to each person. For most, there are multiple things they are committed to. One of them might be going back to school so you can have a better career. Another might be building and sustaining friendships. It could be as straight-forward as taking up a sport, hobby, or instrument and sticking to it through mastery.

They are faithful to their families by being present, loving, and involved parents. To their spouses or partners, being faithful goes beyond not cheating. It means more than just enjoying the good times. When the storms come, as they do to us all, you weather them together, side by side. Ultimately, being faithful means giving it your all and not giving up when things get tough.

The marines also have many slogans that reinforce Norse Pagan values. Here are just a few. "Devotion – Loyalty – Pride." Each word signifies a trait of the Old Norse. "Ready for All, Yielding to None. Ready to Fight. Second to None." What better way to describe a Viking going into battle? The list goes on, but I will share one more that speaks to the heart of a marine, a warrior, and a Viking. "Uncommon Valor. Victory to the Bold. Whatever it Takes" [3].

U.S. Navy

The Navy, on the other hand, has no official motto. However, they have an unofficial one, "non-sibi sed patriae." This is, again Latin, for "Not for self, but country." The motto makes the men and women aware of the sacrifice they will face along their journey and reminds them what is at stake. The Vikings were very aware of the dangers surrounding their lives, but they never hesitated to protect their community [1].

Another unofficial motto of the Navy is "Semper Fortis." This is Latin for "Always Courageous." With sailors venturing off to dark and deep oceans for months and years on end, being courageous is an obvious slogan for them [1][2].

The most essential virtue of a Norse Pagan, Viking, was courage. If you want to stand up for yourself and do the things you believe in, you need a great deal of bravery. You may believe that courage is only necessary for battle, but that is not true. When we are up against a difficult situation our minds and emotions internalize it as a battle. No one is physically striking us, but nevertheless, fear creeps in even to the strongest among us.

Fear is a natural and necessary human emotion. What you do in the face of fear is what separates success and failure. If you want to do more than just get by day to day, to rise above the mass of mediocrity, fear cannot stand in your way. For me, and possibly for you, to achieve challenging goals, overcoming fear, and being courageous is the only way to live.

Imagine walking down a narrow silent street, at 3 am, all alone. Closed factories and boarded warehouses rise up on both sides, blocking out the moon's reflection. In near-total darkness, you pass trash-strewn alleys. In the distance, there is the occasional sound of a car passing. Closer by there is the crunch of dry leaves. What caused it? Maybe it's a feral cat or a dog that escaped from its master's yard, or maybe it's someone behind you, getting closer with every step. For most, the experience would give us a shiver or two. It would be scary for anyone. For some though, rational thought would shut down as fear took hold.

For a segment of the population, venturing out and meeting new people feels like walking alone in the dark. Those living in that fear may just sit in their house with a vague sense of security. The simple things they desire are just out of reach. Work and passion, that sweet sensation of sipping a cold brew at a neighbor's barbeque or spending time with coworkers and friends, all take a back seat. The front door is their battleline. For those that suffer from agoraphobia, joining the world is like walking down that abandoned street over and over again.

To conquer their fear, they must commit to the battle, to fight for what they want their life to be. I truly hope your personal battles are not as difficult to overcome, but they might be. Tackling drug addiction, alcoholism, anorexia, or any number of other things can be just as daunting. In The Saga of Harald Hardrade, from Snori Sturluson's Prose Edda,(c. 46) it says, "Thou art managing ill in being so afraid that thou knowest not what to do." In other words: When we do not control our fear, it prevents us from achieving our goals. Whether your goal is gaining control over a phobia, or finding a better job, mastering your fear is a critical component for success. Facing your fear does not mean you have to do it alone. For some, reaching out for help is their first step onto the battlefield.

Vikings were not fearless; they were human beings. What made them consummate warriors is that they faced their fears with courage. Modern Norse Pagans acknowledge their fear and push through with the fortitude of the gods and ancestors behind them. In the U.S. Army field manual FM 90-5 *Jungle Operations* it states, "A man overcome with fear is of little value in any situation." That is just as relevant to the navy as it is to the army. The reality of it is true for anyone "in any situation." Learning to master your fear is not easy, but the rewards for doing so can be great.

U.S. Air Force

The Air Force has their set of mottos to live by as well, which includes "Aim High." As direct as it is for pilots' slogan to reach higher skies, the motto is deeper than just being a pun. To strive for a better life and fight for a brighter future is a Norse way of life [1].

An individual must have lofty dreams to achieve great things. Without strong motivation, a person will not be able to maintain the effort required to achieve success. For everything that you do, you need to do it with pride and to the best of your abilities. In the old era, a lazy or fearful person was looked down upon by the Nordic gods. The gods discouraged such a lifestyle. We can extrapolate that through their actions. Being mediocre is not the bar a Norse Pagan sets. In all they do, they endeavor to be their best self.

U.S. Coast Guard

Latin mottos do not end there. The Coast Guard's motto is "Semper Paratus" or in English "Always Ready." They would be the first in line if disaster struck in American waters. The slogan carries important sentiment. Even if there are difficult rescues, long hours, and thundering waves, the U.S Coast Guard is always ready to act [1].

The Vikings were sailors. They forged their way through turbulent and freezing Northern waters, to countless countries. The ocean is a cruel monster with no sympathy for any man. It drowns and devours everything. The difficulties faced during Coast Guard rescues, and perilous pursuits of smugglers are a modern-day version of the perils faced by Viking explorers, venturing out through storms and rough seas to unknown lands.

U.S. Army

The army has a great number of mottos and slogans that are there to boost the morale of the individual soldier. The army's official motto is "This We'll Defend," which shows a clear sense of purpose, to safeguard those they are responsible to protect. Loyalty, Duty, Respect, Selfless-Service, Honor, Integrity, Personal Courage" are the official Army values. These are the same ideals expounded on in the Old Norse Hávamál [1][4].

The Norse people were very resilient; it was essential for survival. It showed in every aspect of their lives from making fire, hunting, and building in the frozen North, to sailing out on the open sea in a shallow boat, and fighting, with their bare hands if needed, in order to attain success. In times of adversity, we need to remember that goals can only be achieved if you stay committed to them and do not give up. Like lighting a fire without a match, the task will be laborious, but the reward is well worth the effort.

The famous World War II commander, General George Patton, encouraged the troops to "Accept the challenges so that you can feel the exhilaration of victory." He also said, "If a man does his best, what else is there?" These are not only the fundamental values of the army but also central to the Old Norse lifestyle [4].

Honor is not an act, but a title granted to those who manifest that ideal. An honorable person is courageous and stands up for what they believe in. They live a life true to themselves and an inspiration to others. The Old Norse lived life with a purpose. When their lives ended, they died having no regrets.

The military admires and encourages the same virtues that the Norse people lived by many centuries ago.

Militaries Around the World

It is not just the US military that shares values with the Vikings. "Better to die than to be a coward" is the slogan of The British Royal Gurkha Rifles. They are a one-of-a-kind unit, recruited entirely from Nepal, which is not politically tied to the United Kingdom. They are considered, "amongst the finest and most feared soldiers in the world. They could easily be compared with ancient fighters called the Varangians, predominantly from Sweden, who traveled to the Byzantine territory, modern-day Turkey, beginning in 950 CE. They indenture themselves to the Emperor, for four years, after which a fresh group of Varangians arrived, and the previous fighters returned home. They were considered the best trained and fiercest soldiers in the Roman Empire"

[5] [6].

Here is just a sampling of other military units from across the globe with mottos or slogans that epitomize Old Norse values.

Australia: The Royal Australian Air Force's official motto brings up images of warriors dreaming of Valhalla. "*Per ardua ad astra.*" Which is Latin for, "through adversity to the stars." United Kingdom's Royal Air Force shares that same motto.

Canada: the 2nd Canadian Mechanized Brigade Group's slogan mirrors Norse Pagan mores. *"Audacia et fortitude,"* which is Latin for "Strength and Courage."

France: 1st Marine Infantry Parachute Regiment's slogan is a truism they share with the Vikings of old. *Qui ose gagne,* French for "who dares wins."

India: The Rajputana Rifles, motto restates an argument I have already made. The original is in Sanskrit, "Veer bhogya vasundhara," which translates to, "The Brave shall inherit the earth."

Israel: The General Staff Reconnaissance Unit, Sayeret Matkal, has a motto that closely aligns with the one from India. *"Mi Sheme'ez, Menatze'ah,"* which means "He who dares wins." The Vikings discovered the truth of that maxim a thousand years ago. Their ancestors knew it a thousand years before that.

New Zealand: The 5th Regiment, Wellington's Rifles, has an axiom worthy of Viking praise. It is one that successful people in every field would agree with, "Virtutis Fortuna Comes," Latin for "Good fortune is the companion of courage" [7].

Norse pagans go on the offense instead of waiting with the defense. What are the traits the ancient Norse admired? The list is long, but being courageous, setting lofty goals, and personal expectations, and remaining faithful to them, are definitely in the lineup. In *Germania*, Tacitus writes, "their generals command less through the force of authority, then of example. If they are daring, adventurous, and conspicuous in action, they procure obedience from the admiration they inspire" [8].

As we have seen, the lessons taught through their pagan ways of life are still present in our modern-day society, and the military is a great example of it. If Norse Pagan's values are preserved by the military, then Norse nomenclature and stories are preserved by the media. From books to tv shows, Norse mythology has inspired modern pop culture.

Unless you were born, raised, and continue to live without access to television, radio, books, movies, or the internet, you most likely have heard some about Norse gods.

The Norse Pantheon consisted of many gods with different epithets, abilities, and warrior stories. Besides the gods, the lore is full of harrowing monsters and unearthly creatures. Modern-day media has used these magnificent characters to create interesting stories, music, and visual art. Some famous examples of pop fiction and modern media using Norse Mythology are discussed below.

Norse Mythology in Modern Times

Comic Books

Thor is one of the main characters in Marvel Comics, The Avengers. He was there in the first issue, "The Avengers #1." Captain America didn't show up until issue #4! Thor made his first appearance in comics in 1962, with Journey into Mystery #83.

Marvel comics have gotten inspiration for many of its characters from the Norse pantheon of gods, such as Odin, Loki, Heimdall, and Freyja; the list goes on. It's not just the gods from the far North that jumped into the comic book world. There are also other characters that the Old Norse would recognize, although not in that form, such as the fierce wolf, Fenrir, or the Valkyrie, based on the Old Norse Valkyrie, Brynhildr. She first appears in The Avengers #83 (1970). She was on the "Defender's team" and was even Thor's girlfriend for a time.

Loki is the ultimate trickster. That is true in both Norse Mythology and contemporary depictions of him across the spectrum from comics to movies. The first comic Loki appeared in was way back in 1949 in Venus #6. According to the entertainment website IGN, in 2009, "Loki was ranked eighth-greatest comic book villain of all time" and in 2014 was ranked again by IGN, this time as the "fourth-greatest comic book villain of all time" [11].

European comics

The famous Danish series, *Valhalla,* and the Belgium comic, *Thorgal,* both take inspiration from Norse mythology [12].

Novels

J.R.R Tolkien's critically acclaimed and much-loved novel, *The Lord of the Rings,* and its predecessor, *The Hobbit,* drew influence from many cultures, but the most notable one was Norse mythology. Tolkien used names directly from Prose Edda, such as the sage-like character, *Gandalf,* which is also the name of a dwarf in Norse mythology.

The legend of the *Völsunga Saga,* written in the 13th-century, mentions a magical ring, *Andvaranaut,* that possessed the power to produce gold. It was the inspiration behind the "One Ring," in Tolkien's stories.

Gandalf himself was a wise wizard, inspired by the Norse god, Odin. Middle earth, where mortal men live in Tolkien's world, was geographically inspired by Midgard, the realm in which all humans reside. Elves are superhuman-like beings derived from Norse folklore. In addition, Tolkien used the Norse runic system as inspiration for the legendarium [13].

There are many other fiction writers who took inspiration from Norse mythology. The trilogy series by David Drake, *Northworld*, melds Norse mythology and science fiction together. The world-famous J.K Rowling's *Harry Potter* series took names from Norse folklore such as Death Eater, Fenrir Greyback, and Thorfinn Rowle. Neil Gaiman's graphic novel series, *American Gods,* has characters corresponding to many Norse Gods. This is just a small sampling, but the list goes on and on [12].

Manga and Anime

Attack on Titan is at the top of modern-day anime. It uses Norse themes such as Castle Utgard and Ymir. The plot mimics the storyline from many Norse myths. There is a fight between the titan shifters and non-shifters in the series, which is a reflection of the Aesir and Vanir conflict detailed in the Poetic Edda [12].

Music

Viking metal music is a genre that is popular across Northern Europe. If you like the way heavy metal music pulsates through your whole body, you are going to love this music. From Sweden, you have the bands *Bathory, Thyrfing, Vintersorg,* and *Amon Amarth,* who just came out with a new album, *Berserker.* That's about as Viking as you can get! From Norway, there is *Enslaved, Borknagar,* and *Einherjer.* Other great Viking metal bands are *Týr* from the Faroe Islands,

Moonsorrow from Finland, and *Heidevolk* from the Netherlands.

There are also bands that mix Viking metal and Norse folk music for a powerful combination. *Asmegin* from Norway, *Falkenbach* from Germany, and *Turisas* from Finland are just a few great examples. If metal music isn't for you there are plenty of Viking/Norse folk bands.

In Germany, a pagan folk band named *Faun* produces music you want to sing along to even if you don't know the words. They have an album, *Buch der Balladen*, which contains stories from Norse folklore. They also released a song named *Midgard* and another, *Iduna*, she is the goddess whose apples keep the gods young.

Lady of the Dawn performs both Norse and Celtic folk music that is hauntingly beautiful. Another Norse folk band you don't want to miss is *Skáld*. It is the kind of music that you can't sit still and listen to. Your body is going to move whether you want to or not.

Russian bands, such as *Troll Bends Fir*, and *Nordverg*, also use Norse folklore as themes in their music. In addition to the shared Old Norse influence, most of these bands have another thing in common. They put out great music videos. They are worth checking out for the sets and costumes alone [12].

There are other bands that don't play exclusively Viking music, but they have put out a song or two based on Norse mythology. World-renowned band, *Led Zeppelin* released *Immigrant Song*. *Jethro Tull* put out *Cold Winds to Valhalla*. *Uriah Heep* has a song called *Rainbow Demon*, which was inspired by the Bifrost Bridge and its guard, the god Heimdall, just to name a few [12].

Television Shows

A Norwegian Netflix show called *Ragnarok* is based on a boy that finds out he is Thor himself after fighting with frost giants in Edda. A Danish series called *Jul I Valhal* references lots of the gods in Norse Mythology including Loki. *The Last Kingdom is* a show about the Vikings, told from the point of view of the people they invaded. *Vikings* is a popular action-drama that focuses on the life and family of Ragnar Lothbrok. The character Ragnar is based on Ragnarr Loðbrók whose story is told in the *Gesta Danorum* by Saxo Grammaticus, in the twelfth century. If comedy is more to your liking, there is a series from New Zealand called, *The Almighty Johnsons*. It is based on a family, the Johnson's, who are all reincarnations of Norse gods [12][14].

There are also shows that are not specifically about Norse mythology but have some characters inspired by it or episodes that relate to it. The long-running British TV show, *Doctor Who,* has episodes in which the title character has dealings with some of the Norse gods. The American TV show, *Super-natural*, includes mainly Christian-based deities and demons but has references to Norse characters as well. In the show, Stargate SG-1, there was an entire race of beings called the Asgards [12].

Cartoons

The old cartoon series He-man and new series She-ra, both made by Filmation studio, embodies Norse tradition such as honoring the dead, magic and divination, and weaponry. Freya is shown in the series providing guidance and wisdom to the protagonists. The reboot of Ducktails had an episode called Rumble for Ragnarok. This was a wrestling tournament being conducted in Valhalla to decide the fate of the earth [12].

Films

There are comedy, drama, and action movies based on the Vikings and Norse mythology. Often, they contain elements of all three. In the film *The Mask*, Jim Carey's character finds a mask that is made by Loki, which shapeshifts him and makes him extremely difficult to deal with. The Marvel comic book series has been adapted to films numerous times. Not all of them are relevant here but several, specifically the Avengers series have Norse characters in starring roles.

The kid's movie, *How to Train Your Dragon* (2010), a computer-animated film that takes place in the Viking era, tells the story from a child's perspective. There are other Family-friendly movies that include Vikings or Norse Mythology, for example, *Valhalla* (animated) (1986), *Erik the Viking* (1989), The Island at the Top of the World (2008), and *Valhalla: The Legend of Thor* (2019).

There are also Action-Adventure movies based, at least partly, on Norse Mythology. With this category, horror may be in the mix. In addition to Marvel's movies, there is also *Hammer of the Gods* (2013), *Draug* (2018), and *Midsommar* (2019).

Many period action movies depict Vikings, during the Viking Era including some Icelandic films. Here are some examples from the action-adventure genre: *The Vikings* (1958), *Erik the Conqueror* (1961), *Outlaw: The Saga of Gisli* (1981), *When Ravens Fly* (1984), and *Viking* (2016).

Several dramatic movies attempt to show life as it was in the Viking Era. Of course, any movie that involves Vikings is going to include action as well. Examples are *Shadow of the Raven* (1988), *The White Viking* (1991), and The Legend of Redbad (2019).

Then there are the Viking movies that do not fit neatly into any category such as *The 13th Warrior* (1999) and *Outlander* (2008) [15].

On a more historical note, the film industry has gone back to the Vikings and Norse mythology for inspiration since almost the beginning of the genre. The first was in 1922, with the silent film, *En vikingafilm*. It is about a young man in the hospital recovering from an accident who experiences vivid dreams of being a Viking. The movie *The Viking* (1928) was ahead of its time. Produced during the Silent Era, it was the first full-length movie filmed in Technicolor [16].

Video Games

Hundreds of video games have taken Norse stories, characters, and gods as their themes. In *Tomb Raider*, the protagonist Lara Croft goes to Niflheim and uses Norse artifacts to help find her mother [12].

Dungeons and Dragons have now included Norse Gods in their role-playing game. *Final Fantasy* series is a worldwide played game with characters summoning Odin for guidance, and the setting is in Valhalla and Ragnarok. *Neverwinter Nights* and *Assassin's Creed* are also some games that have had Norse influence [12].

Norse Paganism in Modern Life

Strong men and women are drawn to the values of Norse Paganism. Courage, independence, and resiliency were just some of the qualities of the Vikings. Today, we can focus on those virtues and make positive changes in our life. The Vikings were human, but today they are seen as almost mythological beings. That is because we have lost our connection to them. Most groups can trace their cultural changes step by step.

In the thousand years since the end of the Viking Age, Western Civilization transformed. It went from the Middle Ages into the Renaissance. Then revolutions erupted in the colonies and across Europe which led to the beginning of modern democracy. Next came the Industrial Revolution and with it a massive increase in the wealth of a select few. It also led to an explosion in the number of people enslaved to harvest the raw ingredients needed to make those products which in turn created more wealth.

The riches of people like the Rockefellers created the Gilded Age of overindulgence followed by the devastation of the Great Depression. Wars shaped much of the 1900s. The aftermath of WWI gave rise to WWII. The 1960s and 70s were a time of cultural revolution. Then we had the Cold War and War on Terror. Each of these time periods, and many more left unmentioned, changed society. Over time those changes created a new set of norms. It is how societies have evolved, or devolved, since the first democracy in ancient Greece.

The Viking Age ended a millennia ago, before 1100 CE. It did not come back in a noticeable way until the 1970s when a small group of people in Iceland came together to celebrate the Summer Solstice in 1972. They then formed the first official modern Norse Pagan religion, Íslenska Ásatrúarfélagið. Which in English we refer to as Ásatrú. It was officially recognized as a religion in Iceland in 1973 [17].

It was a great thing in many ways. Being recognized by a national government gave Norse Paganism some legitimacy. People, especially in Europe and the US, became curious and started to learn about the belief system of the Old Norse. It became a legitimate course of study. The ancient books, which will be discussed in a later chapter, were translated into versions that the average person could understand.

There are two big downsides though. First, prior to 1973, it was never an organized religion. The belief system had no set doctrine. It was much more fluid. Depending on the place, the people, and the situation, certain aspects of their creed came to the forefront, and others receded. It was passed on orally. That alone means that it changed over time and place. It would be impossible for every story to be recited identically across a large area of land, through countries with different languages, over the course of hundreds of years. In addition to that, many of the stories that were eventually scribed onto vellum have been partially or completely lost. Others were most likely never written down in the first place. The second problem is far more troubling and will be discussed in a later chapter. It is the issue of racism that has seeped into Asatru [17].

It is important to acknowledge that if, like other cultures and societies, Norse Paganism had been allowed to openly survive and evolve it would have changed as well. Their base values would be the same but historical events and changing social mores would have transformed it into a belief system compatible with modern society.

So, what does it mean to be a Norse Pagan today? It is not a question with a simple or singular answer. It is different for every person. We can look to the Vikings and their connections to the gods for attitudes on traits like courage, self-sacrifice, and faithfulness. At the same time disregard, long outdated beliefs like pillaging churches was alright because they were easy targets. The same line of thought was embraced by other religions. Church leaders no longer call for someone to be burned at the stake.

Looking at military mottos gives us a starting point to delve into Old Norse ideals. That doesn't mean we should all be soldiers or that the various service branches were based on that ideology. The comparison is useful in showing how those values held by the Norse in ancient times might have evolved to be beneficial to us today.

Pointing out the ways the Vikings and Norse mythology has been represented in multi-media serves dual purposes. Even if you don't worship the Norse pantheon of gods, you are most likely more familiar with them than you previously thought. The main reason though is that Norse Paganism is not a religion where you dress fancy one day a week and go listen to someone preach for a couple of hours. It is a way of life. Part of daily life now is going to movies, hanging out, watching television, and listening to music.

The people originally living within the Norse system of beliefs did not give it a name, because it was not a separate thing. It was their way of life. Elements of it permeated every-thing. It swirled around them every day, every hour and minute of their life. It was only with the introduction of Christianity that it was given a word, a designation. Then they referred to it as Forn siðr, which means "old customs," or "the old way." It was a way to distinguish the old way of life, Forn siðr, from the new, Christianity.

What we know about them, and their beliefs comes to us from several sources. Which we will delve into in the next chapter.

Chapter 2
The Sources of Norse Pagan
Myth and Lore

Viewing History within the Context of the Times

There is no written source, directly from the Old Norse, on Norse Paganism. Every source that we currently have has been written by an outsider. What they wrote was influenced by their Christian beliefs. Each of the main sources wrote about their subject with bias, whether conscious or not. In order to get to the "true beliefs" of the Old Norse, as much as that is possible, we need to acknowledge and separate the viewpoint of the authors from the real life of the people they wrote about.

It is not only the original writers that bring bias to the subject of Norse Paganism. As students of history, we do as well. It is important to view cultural events, customs, and beliefs from within the framework of the society in which they occurred. To do less gives a skewed perspective regarding the actions of individuals and groups.

Viewing historical events within the context of the time is something that people too often don't think about. They project our current social ideals onto past people and events, and it skews the reality of what took place during those times. This is currently a contentious issue, and I am not going to get into a diatribe about cultural relativism. In my view, when discussing events from the past it is important to see the world through the eyes of those who lived it. If the norms of the era allowed for certain behavior, how we view it needs to take that social acceptance into consideration. That is especially true when talking about people who lived at least forty generations ago.

Let's look back at a time far closer to our own, the 1930s. Children were seen as a resource and labor. Kids as young as five woke up before dawn to begin their chores. They were expected to put in a couple of hours of hard work before going to school. Many then had to walk miles each way to get an education. Spring Break and Summer vacation were started not as a time to get out of town and have fun, but out of necessity. During harvest season, too many parents kept their children home from school because they were needed as laborers to work on the family farm. Some children never went far enough in school to be fully literate. They had to drop out at a young age to help support their family.

If you look at it through the lens of current values, it would be labeled child abuse. Regardless of whether it was right or wrong, you need to understand that it was a common practice, and most people desperately needed the help. It becomes even more understandable when we add just one piece of information specific to that period of time. The Great Depression began in 1929. Putting events in historical context gives them more meaning, and it is easier to understand why people did what they did.

Another example would be the 1950s when society did not think of women as independent or strong. They were told constantly within the culture to be docile and weak. Women who were obedient and acted almost child-like towards their husbands were far more appreciated. They were expected to do all the housework and child-rearing, without any ambition for something more or different. That is obviously no longer the case. If you look back at a 1950s working woman, now knowing the obstacles she faced, you should have renewed admiration and respect for her and her achievements.

You can see how societal values shift dramatically within a few decades. Keep this in mind when viewing the Viking Era, which existed between roughly 800 CE to 1100 CE. Then, the values and environment were so different that it would be extremely difficult to even envision it. Your feelings towards a person, an event, or activity change when you place them in different timelines. This goes for rituals as well. Presently, religious communities do not sacrifice animals or people. It was common in ancient days but has died out, and for good reasons. Even though there was an element of sacrifice in virtually all religions of the world, we do not do them in the same way the people of old did. Communion took the place of animal sacrifice. For pagans, "sacrifice" is now done by giving food, flowers, alcohol, etc. For example, lots of modern Norse Pagans offer beer or mead to please the god Odin, the All-Father. Today, passing them around to everyone to take a drink and then pouring spirits on the ground, or altar if present, is a form of oblation to the gods.

People who lived one thousand years ago lived life in fear. It is human nature to try and understand why things are the way they are. From prehistory through the Middle Ages and beyond people searched but had few answers to explain the mysteries of the world. They adopted myths and stories to curb their curiosity and find meaning in their suffering. Norse Paganism is rooted in ancient practices and beliefs. It thrives today, but not without adaptation to the modern world. There are two ways to adapt and evolve. The first is to deviate from your core values and give up your identity for the sake of survival. At the time of widespread conversion across Scandinavia, that did in fact happen. In the present day, our religious beliefs are no longer dictated by the state [18].

For those of us inspired by Forn Siðr, the old ways, there is a second method of adaptation we can use. That is to permit the modern world in, allowing us to express the foundational beliefs and traditions in our own unique way. The difference between Norse Paganism in ancient times and the modern world is not a shift in core values. Instead, it is an evolution, acknowledging advances in science and social norms, to meet the needs of heathens in the modern world.

Authors of the Nordic Past and the Words They Wrote

When I first began to learn about Norse Paganism, I found the wide range of terms used for the same group of people sometimes confusing. I did not have a clear idea of how the people from one source were related to the people in another. Even the names of the gods were different depending on whether I was reading from Germania or the Prose Edda. Over time I learned more about who wrote them and the time and circumstances in which they were written. I never found one place where it was all put together so that I could see the larger picture. So, I decided to do that for you here.

Snorri Sturluson and the Prose Edda

One of the main sources of information on Norse Mythology is the Prose Edda, written by the Icelandic author, poet, and wealthy politician, Snorri Sturluson. It was written in the first half of the 13th century, approximately 150 years after Iceland became a "Christian" country. There are four parts to the Prose Edda. It begins with a prologue followed by three sections. The first section, Gylfaginning, contains a multitude of myths from the creation of the worlds to the destruction at Ragnarök. The next section Skáldskaparmál, which means the language of poetry, introduces a wide range of Norse gods. The final section, Háttatal, meaning tally of meters, is one long 20,000-word poem with 102 stanzas. All of which is written in praise of Iceland's ruler at that time, King Hákon of Norway [19][20].

Who was Snorri Sturluson? He was a Christian, writing about the myths and lore of his pagan ancestors. As was common at the time, his prose and poetry were written on sheets of vellum made from calfskin. Despite his own religious beliefs, he wrote in-depth about the pagan past of his people. Today, that doesn't seem unusual. Modern historians write volumes about cultures and beliefs of the past. That was not the case however in the thirteenth century.

The focus of writing that came from Europe at that time was overwhelmingly about Christianity, praise, worship, and admonishments on how to live a Christian life. Writers from Iceland were the exception. Snorri wrote a large body of text about the Pre-Christian Norse, for which we owe him a great debt of gratitude. Current Norse scholars are quick to point out however that his Christian beliefs influenced his retellings. Still, his writings are a rich source of information. Luckily for us, his life was well documented. Snorri was a multi-faceted man as you will come to learn.

He was an aristocratic layman that focused on writing about secular subjects. Born in western Iceland in 1178, he was the son of a chieftain, Hvamms-Sturla. Their family name was used to define a historical period that preceded the loss of political independence in 1262. This period is known as the "Age of Sturlungs" partly because of the great Icelandic saga writing that took place in those years.

At three years old, after his father's death, he was sent to be educated and raised in Oddi, located in Southern Iceland, under another chieftain Jón Loptsson. This person, who tutored Snorri, was a deacon and a member of the resistance against an expansion of the church's power. Here, Snorri became an educated writer. His learning came predominantly from the native literature of his people and not from continental European books which were mainly written in Latin.

He married into a wealthy family when he was twenty years old. At that time, he started living part-time in the town of Borge in Western Iceland. It was where his wife grew up. Her father owned valuable property in the area. After his father-in-law's death, he went to permanently live there in 1202. Later, using his wealth and inheritance, Snorri bought several pieces of land in the greater Borgarfjörður area. Over a relatively short period of time, he was able to acquire many highly sought-after properties in various parts of Iceland. According to historical records, he also controlled some church properties that served to increase his power and influence [19].

His wife, Herdís, bore him two children, but they died in 1233. Snorri was not a faithful husband. He sired several children out of wedlock. He openly claimed his illegitimate offspring. They carried his name and one son, at least, followed in his political footsteps. Snorri became a wealthy and powerful man who was not above using intimidation to get what he wanted. His method, of acquiring land and chieftaincies, was also done by other wealthy people, leaving thirteen-century Iceland at the mercy of a few rich families, including Snorri Sturluson's.

Snorri, at his peak, used his position and contacts to exploit people. There were ongoing disputes between the small group of wealthy landowners. Iceland did not have a monarchy. There was not a singular leader in the country, but each of the powerful men wanted to be the one that came out on top, able to claim the role. In their quest for personal gain, they lost sight of the bigger picture and Iceland ended up under the rule of the Danish king [19].

Snorri Sturluson was the president or law speaker for the Alþingi, the General Assembly of Iceland, twice, from 1215 to 1218 and again from 1222 to 1231. In a nod to self-importance, Snorri named his booth at the General Assembly, Valhöll, after the mythological hall in Asgard where all of Odin's fallen warriors are believed to reside. Other than a forty-four-year period from 1800 to 1843 when Denmark forced its closure, the Alþingi has been at the center of Iceland's government since 930 CE [21].

Snorri also sent his son to make good connections and gain favor with the king of Norway, who was ruling Iceland at the time. Meanwhile, he continued to gain resources and influence in his homeland. In 1224, he started a partnership with the wealthiest woman in Iceland. It is unknown whether they were a couple or strictly business associates, but there is no evidence of him being in another relationship after meeting her.

He was at one point the richest and most powerful man in Iceland. With so much power, he got greedy, and in 1240, he rebelled against the king of Norway in an attempt to become the king of Iceland himself. His fall from paramountcy was dramatic. In 1241, one of his rivals sent men after Snorri, who took refuge in a wine cellar, where he was found and murdered. His murder was ordered by none other than King Hákon of Norway, the monarch he praise for 102 stanzas in the Háttatal [19].

Historians may question Snorri's integrity and character based on documented evidence of how he treated others. But there is no question as to his importance from a literary standpoint. In addition to preserving stories that might otherwise have been lost to the annals of history, he published hundreds of poems and introduced verse and meter forms to Icelandic poets. There is no doubt that Snorri was a Christian, but instead of superiority or scorn, he wrote 'heathen' stories from the perspective of the Norse pagans. He imbibed them with vivid details while utilizing expressive kennings and humor.

Poets and storytellers were held in high regard in Scandinavia throughout the Old Norse Era. In addition to Snorri's financial and political ambitions, he also set his sights on becoming an acclaimed poet. Luckily for us, he succeeded in that endeavor as well. His Prose Edda is a rich source of Old Norse mythology and lore [20].

Titles can be a little confusing. Snorri Sturluson was a poet, but the literary work he is known for is the Prose Edda. The Poetic Edda is an entirely different book. It was written by multiple people, but Snorri was not one of them.

Poetic Edda, Authors Unknown

The Poetic Edda is a compilation of what were originally more than thirty poems written by anonymous authors; twenty-nine of the poems have survived to modern times. The work was compiled in the late thirteenth century. It is also called the Codex Regius, or more accurately, the Codex Regius of the Poetic Edda. It was given that name when it was gifted to the King of Denmark. Codex Regius means something like "Book of the King." The Poetic Edda is known by several names: Poetic Edda, Codex Regius, Codex Regius of the Poetic Edda, Elder Edda, and Sæmundar Edda. Most people refer to it as the Poetic Edda. To avoid confusion, that is the term that I will use as well.

In 1936 Henry Adams Bellows translated The Poetic Edda into English. Although parts had been translated in English prior to Bellows, his version is considered by many scholars to be the first complete and accurate version. In the Introduction to that translation, he wrote:

"The Poetic Edda is the original storehouse of Germanic mythology. It is, in many ways, the greatest literary monument preserved to us out of the antiquity of the kindred races which we call Germanic."

Bellows goes on with grandiose praise. For example, Völuspá contains, "one of the vastest conceptions of the creation and ultimate destruction of the world ever crystallized in literary form." The Hávamál, "can bear comparison with most of the

Biblical Book of Proverbs," and Thrymskviða, "contains one of the finest ballads in the world." His praise may seem over the top, but each time I read from the Poetic Edda I can't help but agree with him [22].

The "Poetic Edda" was given the name "Edda" because of its similarity to the content and period of Snorri's Edda. Also, like Snorri's, it was written on Vellum. Based on the handwriting, experts agree that the initial Poetic Edda was transcribed by a single person. Who that person was is as mysterious as the authors of the individual stories he collected. The only thing we know for sure is that the person was a man. Women were not allowed to be scribes at that time.

The original Poetic Edda is housed at the Arni Magnusson Institute, in Iceland. All contemporary Norse Pagans owe a debt of gratitude to Arni Magnusson. He was an Icelandic scholar in the later thirteenth century. He made it his mission in life to collect and preserve as many of the earlier writings from his country as he could find. The Poetic Edda was one of those finds. He left Iceland and became a professor at the University of Copenhagen. He left his entire collection to the university upon his death. It remained in Denmark until the Danish parliament passed an act returning Magnusson's collected works to Iceland. The act was passed in 1961 but it took another ten years for the original Poetic Edda to be returned to Iceland. It is only fitting that its final resting place is named after the man who saved it from obscurity [21][23].

The Icelandic Sagas

The information about the origin of the Icelandic Sagas is sparse at best. That doesn't detract in any way though from the rich and dramatic stories they contain. Icelandic Sagas are an important source of Norse pagan history. A saga is a series of semi-historical stories put together in a cohesive way about an important person, usually a king. These stories give us a fuller picture of the influential people in early Icelandic history. They also tell of the difficulties 2nd and 3rd generation Norse and Celtic settlers to Iceland experienced. All of the sagas come from the time of the Old Norse, before and through the Viking Age. They are eventually written down by a variety of authors during the 13th and 14th centuries. When reading the sagas, it is important to know that at that time, medieval Iceland did not have a centralized authority. There were though plenty of laws and legal traditions.

The men and women described in the sagas are relatable. Despite the massive cultural differences, their struggles feel very close to home. Their lives and deaths both leave a mark on the reader. The sagas are filled with action and drama. They contain no observations or analyses concerning ethics. The stories are presented without moral commentary. The saga's style and characteristics make it unique. In contrast,

Middle Ages Latin used lengthy prose to discuss morality. The sagas are written in the colloquial language spoken by everyday Icelandic Norseman at that time.

One story told within the sagas is of the Viking king, Haskulf, who came back to his recently captured land in hope of retaking it. He was asked by his Irish captors if he wanted to be ransomed but replied with smug bravado. Announcing that he would come back with even more warriors if he was returned. He was beheaded shortly thereafter [24].

Völsunga Saga, The Saga of the Völsungs, tells the story of a family through multiple generations. Many of the actions perpetrated by the various characters will seem overly violent, without concern for human life. This is a good example of the importance of looking at things within context. Iceland is a brutally cold, unforgiving land, with few natural resources. In the Middle Ages, the most important group to anyone was their family. No one could survive alone. Big towns were nonexistent. Small groups of people, families through blood or marriage, were constantly fighting with neighboring groups for the few resources available. It was truly a time of survival of the fittest. Taking care of, and backing up, your family was the most important thing people did [25].

The sagas also have lifeless paragraphs that present the genealogies of the leaders. This reflects the importance of remembering ancestors, which every chieftain was required to do. It is not known whether or not reciting the genealogy of important people was done when it was only an oral tradition. Some scholars think that the practice was influenced by Christianity, specifically the long lists of who begat who, from the Old Testament.

All of the northern peoples loved to tell the saga stories. Many of the Norse tales were later written down by English, Roman, and even Russian historians. Just because the sagas were first written down in Iceland does not mean that they all originated there. It is possible that some of the Icelandic sagas actually originated in Sweden but were not put into writing until the story made its way to Iceland.

The Swedish runic stone Rök, sometimes referred to as "a library in stone," may actually be an example of this. Its ancient songs and writings are very similar to the Icelandic Saga, Fornaldarsǫgur. In the saga itself, it tells of a merchant from Iceland who heard the stories at the Swedish king's court. Maybe this is evidence that, in the Swedish court, the saga was recited although never written down.

The saga style of storytelling not only belongs to Icelandic people but also to Norwegians. Norsemen, from present-day Norway, have told these stories since ancient times. For example, the book of Icelandic settlers called "Landnámabók" had stories that dated back to the 1st century, hundreds of years before Iceland was discovered. The people of Norway connected these stories and spread them as well.

The saga style is very dramatic, with scattered verses and art. The fairytale-like sentences narrate the life of a hero including important events. Likewise, fairytales are very much to the point. They do not diverge off into discussions about morality or what motivated a character. A saga is written the same way.

Most of Iceland is inhospitable land. No trees grow there and instead of lakes and rivers they have snow-covered mountains and dangerous ice sheets. The cold, harsh land could not help but influence people's personalities, making them realists, well-disciplined, and calm. There are no beautiful forests to rest or daydream in. The land was far from the happenings of the outside world. This meant that for the most part they did not have the near-constant worry about border skirmishes or wars common in the rest of the world.

Life was difficult. Resources were scarce, but the isolation of Iceland allowed them to live otherwise peaceful lives. The Icelandic Sagas represent this reality and attitude in their prose. They are direct, clear, and without frivolous commentary. These sagas are romantic and historical but not romance or historical pieces. They describe the life of the people in an artistic style. Saga narration in oral traditions originated in ancient pre-Viking settlements. For instructions on how to access all of the Icelandic Sagas online, check out the link in the resource section at the back of the book [24].

Saxo Grammaticus and Gesta Danorum

Also known as the History of Danes, is the largest collection of Norse mythology, consisting of sixteen books, with nine being translated into English. A lot of what we know about Norse Paganism comes from this body of work. This book was written around the 12th century by Saxo Grammaticus. Saxo and Snorri both made references to some stories that historians have been unable to find, in their entirety, anywhere else. This indicates that many stories have been lost in the darkness of time. Every so often old documents and artifacts are found. So, there is always the hope that someday we will have an even fuller picture of the Old Norse lore.

Saxo was born on the island of Zealand. Little is known about his early life. Based on his own writing and that of another writer and nobleman at that time, Sven Aggesen, we know he was a soldier, at least for a while. Both his father and grandfather were soldiers in the service of King Valdemar I of Denmark. He was later a canon to the Lund Cathedral in the late twelfth and early thirteenth centuries. While there he was a secretary to an archbishop, Absalon. It was he who supported and encouraged Saxo to pursue writing and history.

Grammaticus had his own style of writing, not fully in line with other European writers in Latin at that time, but also unlike the unique Icelandic style of writing that Snorri Sturluson implemented. He blended prose stories with poetry. If you know a great deal about poetry and compare the two writers, side by side, you can see the difference in meter and rhythm. Saxo utilizes much of the Latin style. We could go on in a hoity-toity fashion about the finer distinctions in poetry, but it is not necessary to know anything about poetry to enjoy and appreciate the writings of both.

Saxo's first books contain ancient stories, a mixture of myths and legends. These books incorporate tales of heroes and warriors, tender love stories, and beings from another world. Stories about dragons, witches, wizards, and even vampires can be found there. Many of these stories went on to become popular children's fairytales that are still enjoyed by Scandinavian children today.

After the ninth book, he introduced historical figures, talking about the lives of Viking kings and royalty. There is an element of the fairytale in all of his writing, in that he does not concern himself with sticking strictly to fact. He has a clear bias towards Denmark. He also is a strong proponent of Christianity. These two things combine to create a clear sense of right and wrong, good and evil, Christian Danes versus pagan Vikings. This kind of split we typically find more in fairytales than in historical texts. So, it is important to not take everything at face value or as totally factual. His work is not among the best, but it is very important in showing medieval life and how they viewed things. He is also the only historian, whose work has survived, for that particular place and time.

The book, Gesta Danorum, History of the Danes, was written in a narrative style, that is elegant and complex. There is a wide range of topics and tones in his stories. For example, he wrote a funny story about a drunk, trying desperately to get beer despite an alcohol restriction in his town. On the other end of the spectrum, he wrote the first version of the story of Hamlet, made famous by Shakespeare [26][27].

Another prominent source of Norse Pagan insight and history is Germania. It was written by the Roman historian Tacitus in the year 98 CE. Although the names of the gods were different from those their descendants used during the time of the Vikings, it contains the earliest known writings about the Germanic people. Many of their traits, values, and customs remained intact through the Viking period.

Germania: Tacitus' Work and Legacy

The full name of the ancient author is Gaius Cornelius Tacitus. He was an orator and held many public offices. He is referred to as one of the best prose stylists of Latin. He was also a preeminent historian whose writings gave us the earliest glimpse of the Vikings' ancestors.

Apart from Germania, he wrote Historiae, which details events from 69 to 96 CE in the Roman Empire. He also wrote Annals, which describes the Roman Empire from 14 to 68 CE. Current historians have no idea who his parents were, but he grew up privileged with a strong educational background that later helped him in his political career.

Rhetoric at that time was more than just the study of prose composition. It involved learning how to speak to the public, with an attitude of authority, and present an argument to the masses, which Tacitus was schooled in. His later education largely revolved around training needed to get desirable posts within the government. There is one position that stands out in his resume, which possibly influenced his writing of Germania. In his early thirties, he joined another school, not as a student but as a member of the college. It was the institution that kept the Sibylline Books of Prophecy. It also oversaw foreign-cult practices, which would include what was known at that time of the beliefs and rituals of the Germanic people.

He also studied law under Marcus Aper and Julius Secundus. One of his first positions was to be a military tribunate with a Roman legion. He also married an important politician's daughter. This gave him social mobility so that he could move higher up in society than his background might otherwise allow. This further solidified his position in the government. By 93 CE, he had made a name for himself. He was seen as an orator with a solid moral reputation who projected dignity. After becoming a historian, he wrote about the political environment of his time, which included Nero's death [28].

The Germania was named after the place in which the Germanic tribes lived. It was bordered on the west by the Rhine and includes present-day Germany, Poland, the Czech Republic, Slovakia, Hungary, and Austria. Romans called the people "barbarians." Tacitus showed the Germanic tribes' values and virtues, all the while describing Roman's cruelty and lax morality. The tribes were in danger because of the Roman Empire, but they were also a danger to the goal of continued Roman expansion.

Tacitus was a literary stylist; his facts and opinions were presented in an alluring way. Ancient historians often intertwined the facts of a time or event with the opinions and personality of the writer. It was also common to exaggerate human actions or physical abilities. Throughout much of history, facts and myths were often combined in the telling of stories. It was done extensively in the Icelandic Sagas. Saxo Grammaticus did it as well, but Tacitus seems to stick to facts regarding the actions of people. He did not incorporate myth, but he does invoke a level of classical romanticism into his writing. Giving the "barbarians" at times idealized versions of the virtues they possessed [28][29].

Unfortunately for history, some groups have seized on those romanticized versions of the ancient Germanic people. In his comparisons between the two groups, Tacitus implies that the uncivilized Germanic people were morally and ethically superior to the cultured Romans. Setting them up on a pedestal based on their perceived ethics and values. Those groups, from the late nineteenth century to the present, latched onto the idea that with their lighter skin and hair, along with the fact that the average barbarian was larger and stronger than the average Roman, to proclaim the inhabitants of Germania not just remarkable morally, but physically superior as well. They then attached themselves to that Germanic ancestry and proclaimed membership in the "superior race."

The False and Dangerous Use of Germania

Books can be used to spread fear and instill a dangerous mindset among the masses. Fear, in turn, can make people cruel. They demonize "the other," and define them in ways that are no longer human. There are certain books in history that have had a strong and devastating influence on large groups of people.

You probably know about or have at least heard the title of some dangerous books that have done just that, including Hitler's "Mein Kampf," Marx and Engel's "The Communist Manifesto," Mao Zedong's "Quotations from Chairman Mao," or even Freidrich Nietzsche's "Beyond Good and Evil." However, you would not expect a book written by an ancient Roman politician to be considered menacing. According to Harvard professor Christopher Krebs, Germania should also be on the list of the topmost dangerous books.

National Socialism, or Nazism, had many discourses, and Tacitus' writing played a role in shaping many of them. The small, time-worn book was rediscovered in the mid-1800s. At that point, it mainly had a German, humanist readership. Nationalists in the 19th century popularized the book. In the aftermath of World War I, Nazi leaders began to use the ancient text to propagate the idea of a superior German race. Germania was even referred to as the Bible by the foot soldiers of the Nazis.

In order to view the situation clearly, there are certain things you should be aware of. In Germania, Tacitus describes Rome's fiercest enemy, the Germanic barbarians. There is a long, ongoing debate between Old Norse scholars as to whether or not Tacitus actually went to the region, and witnessed with his own eyes, the events he wrote about. It is possible that everything he put in Germania came from his imagination and what he learned at the school where they studied foreign-pagan practices.

Another vital point is that his work describes the unwritten rules the Germanic people lived by. In many ways they were ideals. He also criticized the people, but admiration is clearly present. Tacitus' writings, at the time, could have been an attempt to defend the tribes against the brutality of the Roman Empire. Regardless, the book was written two thousand years ago. To equate modern Germans with the people of Germania is the same as saying first century Christians are the same as those people filling the pews of megachurches today. It is a hard comparison to swallow.

Two thousand years after it was written, the Nazis perpetuated their skewed reading of Tacitus' work to further their racial agenda. The Nationalists' description of Germania leads you to believe that everything the Nazis are associated with came from this book. The book does show the pride of the people that then resided in "Germania." What they choose to ignore are all of the beliefs that don't fit into their ideology. For example, I doubt Nazi leaders kept special white horses so that they could make predictions about the future based on how the animals pranced around a clearing.

Heinrich Himmler, head of the SS, was a fervent occultist. He linked the German people to earth-born humans that descended from gods. He was central to convincing Hitler of the importance of using Germania for the purpose of propaganda. Hitler was not very learned and did not like reading, but thanks to Himmler he learned a convoluted version of the information Germania contained. Although associated with the horrors of World War II, Germania itself is not a dangerous book [30].

The Nazis ignored all history of migration. They also dramatically reduced the physical area that they considered to be Germania. They regarded both Germans and Austrians as descendants of the people that lived in Germania. They did not believe that people in Poland or the Czech Republic were the progeny of the same group, and yet when you look at a map of ancient Germania the landmass contained within its borders encompassed all four of those countries and more. Ultimately, for those who believe the hate-filled racist views held by the Nazis, the assumption will always be that what Tacitus wrote was the complete and accurate truth, at the time he wrote it. Maybe it was.

Unfortunately, what the Nazis and other like-minded groups have done, is to take what the Roman historian wrote and twist it around to fit their agenda. I've read Germania dozens of times, studying every detail. There is nothing in it that supports the Nazi agenda. The next chapter of this book clearly breaks down the racist argument brick by brick. What you are left with is a snapshot in time. People, in this case, White supremacists, look at that picture and then jump to the most improbable explanation for what is supposedly taking place. It is the equivalent of seeing an old photo of a family eating at an Italian restaurant and jumping to the conclusion that the dad must be Al Capone. It really is that ridiculous of a leap, as I will now explain.

Chapter 3
Racism is NOT a part of Norse Paganism

E vents in the United States over the last several years
have brought to the surface of society a problem that
has boiled beneath for quite some time. People use the cloak
of Norse Paganism to propel racist ideology within the framework of a legitimate religious belief. The idea that only
people with "Norse blood" should follow the gods of the
North, is based on a misreading of history and the text.

The Prose Edda makes clear that all people come from the
same source. The god Heimdall, in human form, created the
first human from each class structure. The point here is that
slaves and kings were originally fathered by the same man.
We are all related. It is not where someone was born or the
color of their skin that determines their value. Each person is
responsible for their own actions. Whether they are "good"

by Viking standards depends on how they live their life. Are they good hosts? Do they follow the rule of reciprocity? Are they strong and brave? Are they honest? Do they use good judgment? Are they willing to make sacrifices in order to achieve their goals? Do they honor the gods and their ancestors? Do they follow the "rules" for dealing with other creatures and the unseen world? Those are just some of the things that are considered in determining a person's worth in Norse pagan society.

People often use the terms Norse Pagan and Ásatrú interchangeably. To equate Norse pagans and heathens with Ásatrú is a mistake. It is a minor group in the pagan world. Although I have seen no evidence that the religion was formed with a racist ideology, it has attracted a "folk" element that believes in excluding all people whose ancestry is not Northern European. The religion has done little beyond lip service to dissuade that way of thinking. Therefore, the organized religion of Ásatrú is a problematic thing for the majority of pagans and heathens.

Racists in Ásatrú and What Modern Heathens are Doing about It

Around the world, white supremacists use Norse pagan symbols in their demonstrations and protests. In 2017, they protested in Charlottesville, Virginia at the Unite the Right

Rally. Nazi and Confederate flags were proudly carried through the streets. Also present, to the horror of Norse Pagans and followers of Ásatrú, was the valknut. It is an ancient Germanic symbol said to represent Odin.

It is made up of three interconnecting triangles. There are numerous examples of it carved into rocks at ancient Germanic archeological sites. It is rightly a part of the heathen lexicon. Unfortunately, as with many other Old Norse symbols, such as Thor's hammer, it was usurped by White supremacists.

In Iceland, where the first government-recognized Norse pagan religion, Ásatrú, was founded, the protest in Charlottesville created quite a stir. Hilmar Hilmarsson, a high priest, called a goði, saw those religious symbols used in the protest. He was upset, but not surprised.

"The racist interpretation of heathenry is a total perversion of the original mythology." This misconception is not only present in the U.S. but also in other countries such as Canada, Germany, and Sweden. Unfortunately, when asked what could be done to change that erroneous perception, that excludes non-Northern Europeans from Ásatrú, his response was disheartening. "We don't try to use logic with people who are totally illogical in the first place." His advice on how to deal with this huge and growing problem within Norse paganism can be summed up in two words, ignore it. Not all followers of Ásatrú feel that way. There are some trying to make a difference.

Karl Seigfried is a highly respected writer on Norse mythology and paganism. He is also a *goði* of an inclusive Ásatrú group in Chicago, Thor's Oak Kindred. When asked for his view after the events in Charlottesville, he said, "Those who seek validation for hateful views will always manage to find some passage they can interpret in a way that justifies their bigotry." According to Seigfried, this is true of every religion, polytheistic and monotheistic alike.

His suggestion is that people write theological essays that he can organize and publish as an international anthology for heathens. He hopes to bring in essays on topics from global warming to the role of government based on a close reading of the mythology. I look forward to reading it someday, but at this point, it is still in the planning stages [31].

Others believe that the way to address the hate is to be a visible counterpoint. Diana Paxson, one of the founders of the Alliance for Inclusive Heathenry, puts herself physically on the frontline against racist protestors. "Every time they [White supremacists using heathen symbols] come out with their message, we need to get out there with ours."

Paxson believes that heathenry is a religion that respects the nature and diversity of humankind and encourages active protection of their rights based on the actions of the diverse pantheon.

Another group also believes in protesting against racists whenever they use heathen symbols in bad faith. To save their symbols from being misused, Vikings Against Racism, a group in Sweden, shows up at racist rallies to publicly denounce them. In a recent event, Nordic Resistance Movement, a Nazi group, took the symbol of the god Týr, the rune Tiwaz, as their main logo. The racist group did not intimidate others during the event in the way they had envisioned. Instead, they were outnumbered by members of Vikings Against Racism. The hope is that having other pagans there, presenting an anti-racist perspective alongside the hate-filled propaganda, gives on-lookers a more balanced perspective [31].

Unfortunately, Ásatrú has been adopted by a large number of racists. These people advertise the idea of racism as the central focus of the religion. It is a minor group, but it has done plenty of harm to the heathen community and to perceptions held around the world of who Norse Pagans are and what they believe. As a result of the perceived connection to racists, Nazis, and neo-Nazis, "the reputation of Norse mythology was forever tainted in the eyes of the general public." Racism was never a part of the Old Norse beliefs and does not belong in it now. It will not be a quick or easily won battle to educate the outside world regarding the non-racist roots of heathenry [32].

You might be saying to yourself, "why worry about it? I know who I am as a Norse Pagan." It matters though. In the aftermath of WWII, "Norse mythology became a taboo subject... Due to the fear of being labeled a Nazi sympathizer, scholarly research stagnated; Norse archeological expeditions were defunded..." That stigma persists to this day. If the general public continues to associate Norse Pagans with the Nazis, then all heathens by default are viewed with suspicion no matter how much we as individuals condemn racism. I believe that there are many people who would look deeper into our pagan religion if it were not tainted by the perceived racist connection [32].

This "religion" never has been, nor should it ever be, one with missionaries trying to bring in new converts. However, for those around the world searching for a system of beliefs that fit with how they view their life, the people they love, and the earth in which we all reside, heathenry may very well be the answer they are looking for. Because they are not racist, and would never become involved with any religion or organization that was, many of those people will never look deeper into the Old Norse faith. I find that very disheartening. Not only is it false, but those that believe the lie continue to perpetuate the misconception.

Why "intermarriage" was not seen in *Germania*

In Germania #2 Tacitus writes, "The Germans, I am apt to believe, derive their original from no other people; and are nowise mixed with different nations arriving amongst them." An earlier translation puts it this way, "The Germans themselves I should regard as aboriginal, and not mixed at all with other races through immigration or intercourse" [33][34].

Germania was, intentionally or otherwise, misunderstood and misused by the Nazis of Germany before and during the Second World War. It was the source cited by the Nazis for their stand on racial purity. Their version of the text was that the original people of Germany did not intermarry because they considered themselves an exceptional race. They used the ancient book to justify a belief system they wanted to be enforced. Tacitus' writing continues to be used to promote racist ideas in Norse paganism. That is not how it was written.

The reason Tacitus believed that they were, "not mixed," is because of their physical appearance. "All have fierce blue eyes, red hair, huge frames." That hardly describes the majority of modern-day Germans. Hitler had blue eyes, but that is where the similarities end. His height was never officially released but based on picture comparisons he was most likely between 5'6" and 5'8". That hardly fits Tacitus' description, nor does his stature bring to mind the descendants of those people, that continued to migrate north and west, the Vikings [34][35][36].

We could discuss how the people of Germania mixed and "intermarried" with others over the last 2,000 years, in order to reconcile the differences in the singular look of the ancient people as opposed to the wide variance in the appearance of modern Germanic people. To do so, however, would take us away from the point. In order to move into the meat of the argument, I will take Tacitus' statement at face value. The people of Germania, "appear to me indigenous, and free from intermixture with foreigners." He says this as a statement of fact, not a judgment. The Nazis, and subsequent White Supremacists, conveniently end the quote there. What they and others fail to do is ask the obvious question, "why?"

Why did the people of Germania only have children with other people from Germania? What Tacitus says next is extremely important if our goal is to clarify the situation. "For the emigrants of former ages performed their expeditions not by land, but by water; and that immense, and, if I may so call it, hostile ocean, is rarely navigated by ships from our world." What the author clearly states is that the inhospitable environment in Northern Europe prevented other people from emigrating there. According to Tacitus, the only ones with ships capable of safely coming and going from that part of the world were the indigenous people of the region, the ancestors of the Vikings [33][34].

Tacitus goes on by asking a question of his own, "who would leave Asia, or Africa, or Italy for Germany, with its wild country, its inclement skies, its sullen manners and aspect, unless indeed it were his home?" It is a valid point. In order to put it fully in context, it is important to understand what the land was like. The massive area is described in #5. "Their country... either bristles with forests or reeks with swamps." It is "productive in grain but unkindly to fruit-bearing trees." The people do have livestock, but "these are for the most part undersized." In addition to all that, "silver and gold the gods have refused to them." In #6 we learn "Even iron is not plentiful with them," which prevents them from making weapons that are comparable to the ones produced by the Romans [34].

Tacitus seems to be making the argument that the reason they did not intermix was not that the people of Germania would not allow people from other lands in, rather it was that no one from an area outside of Germania would want to live there. Looking at the situation strictly through the outsider's eyes, what could be gained by joining the people of the North? It would require a level of wealth to get there. At the very least he would need a good boat and enough supplies to make the voyage. He would also need to hire a navigator or risk being lost at sea. For that reason, we can assume that anyone moving North came from a relatively successful background.

If he was used to a comfortable life within the Roman empire he would certainly lose a great deal. In Rome, he would have enjoyed a varied diet that included assorted fruits, vegetables, and dishes made with olive oil and other seasonings. Eating that well in Germania would be out of the question. Even if he arrived with plenty of supplies he would be expected to share them and would not be in a position to refuse. "Cold and hungry they are accustomed by their climate and soil to endure." Within a very short period of time, he too would be cold and hungry.

For all of his money and hardship, what would an outsider hope to gain? "Trade was vital to Ancient Rome. The empire cost a vast sum of money to run and trade brought in much of that money." Expanding trade and increasing the tax base was the main reason Roman legions continued to open up new lands and claim them for Rome. Fragrances, such as "Frankincense and myrrh" were brought in from parts of Africa. "Arab merchants brought these goods to Roman markets by means of camel caravans along the Incense Route." Those same caravans also brought "spices, gold, ivory, pearls, precious stones, and textiles," from "Africa, India, and the Far East." Silk came from China via the Silk Road [37][38].

The Germanic tribes were not the only people from the North. Rome already traded with groups from the Baltic, modern-day Estonia, Latvia, and Lithuania. The area was rich with amber, which they used in medicine and for making jewelry. By the time Tacitus wrote *Germania*, there were 8,000 miles of road in Britain. The main export from there to the Roman Empire was tin. They also exported lead, salt, iron, and copper from the island. Smaller amounts of gold and silver were acquired as well [39][40].

Germania had little to offer in trade. Even the animals were not as good as those commonly found elsewhere in the empire, Tacitus tells us that small herds of the "beeve kind" are the "only species of wealth. Silver and gold the gods... have denied to this country." Not having gold, silver, or precious jewels was not a problem for the Germanic people. "The possession of them is not coveted by these people as it is by us," In addition to the hostile landscape, weather, and meager food, lack of valuable metals to mine kept adventurous gold and silver traders on the Roman side of the Rhine and Danube.

Tacitus tells us that there is "some" gold and silver to be found, mainly as gifts that were given to the chiefs. So perhaps, an adventurous man might think he could get rich and live a great comfortable life by acquiring that wealth the Germanic people did not seem to appreciate anyway. Of course, it would be a fool's endeavor, but for the sake of argument and the lack of any better, let us assume that would be the motivation and move on in our hypothetical journey of adventure [34].

The hopeful foreigner would most assuredly be playing the long game. Such a person would need to ingratiate themselves into the society, become friends with the chief, and somehow convince him that what he had was a worthy trade for the chieftain's wealth. I think it is a reasonable assumption that no one would assume they could simply march in and take it. The reputation of the Germanic people was known across the Roman Empire. All would know that trying to steal from them was a suicide mission. Also, it still would not produce the hereto unseen mixed-blood child.

In order to fully debunk the false argument made by White Supremacists and others, it is important that we carefully analyze every possible reason for why the ancient people did not produce children with outsiders. Their argument is that the Germanic people would not allow it. In fact, the reasons "why" were the exact opposite. No one from the civilized world had any reason to move there, and so they did not. We have talked about how the physical environment was an obstacle to foreigners that might otherwise want to emigrate. Tacitus makes this argument, as well as the next. Germania did not at that time possess any resources that an outsider would want enough to warrant going there. That leaves two options to investigate, love or the desire to live life in the same way the Germanic people did. In some ways, those two reasons could be tied together.

What About Love??

Despite the outward appearance of being a wild, uncivilized people, the Old Norse/Germanic culture was clearly structured, although with different values and customs than the rest of the "civilized" world. The rules were in many ways every bit as defined. In #19, it explains that extramarital affairs were basically unheard of. "Clandestine correspondence is equally unknown to men and women." People did not have sex outside of marriage in that culture. "The loss of chastity meets with no indulgence; neither beauty, youth, nor wealth will procure the culprit a husband... "No one in Germany laughs at vice, nor do they call it the fashion to corrupt and to be corrupted." At that time the women of Germania would not agree to sex outside of marriage. The consequences for doing so were far too high. So, the only way for children of mixed origin to be born would be if their parents were married. It is an important point to make because that was not always the case in Rome at that time [34].

Unlike much of the civilized world, marriages were not arranged between "powers." Up until relatively modern times, a princess could be married off to a prince in a far-off land. Often, they would not meet until their wedding day. The Old Norse had nothing like that in their culture. They married people that they knew, and their parents knew. It was the family that arranged the marriage. You may be thinking, what if an outsider fell in love with a Germanic man or woman? Surely intermixing would happen then. It would have been nearly impossible for a foreigner to come close enough to the Germanic people such that they fell in love with an individual amongst them, but we will set that aside.

For argument's sake, we will concede that a foreign man has seen a Germanic woman from afar, most likely from across the battlefield, and felt the sting of Cupid's arrow. So, our poor lovelorn foreigner devises a plan to be united with the object of his affection. He decides to move into Germania and ask for her hand in marriage. First, he must overcome all of the aforementioned obstacles, lack of access, difficult terrain, and little food. To top it off, he probably did not own clothing adequate to survive a winter in that climate. Remember, this was long before he could order arctic wear online.

Despite all that, let us say that the lovestruck outsider did move into that inhospitable land in the hope of marrying the Germanic woman of his dreams. His next obstacle would be getting her parents' approval. Bravery and self-sacrifice were expected. It would take time for the family and larger community to get to know the newcomer. No family would consent to a daughter marrying someone that was not considered as good as a local man. It would be dishonorable. In that culture, honor was extremely important. A man would fight to the death in order to maintain it.

Would the young woman's family approve of the marriage to an outsider considering the emphasis placed on warring and bravery? Any disapproval of the marriage would come not because he came from some other place but because they did not know enough about his character. It is not realistic that they would give their child to someone they barely knew. It would take time for him to prove himself. How good is he in battle? How does he react to defeat? Is he brave or a coward? It could take years of bravery in battle and in dealing with others at home in Germania before the parents were willing to give consent. The man would have a hard time proving he was worthy of the maiden's hand. It is far more likely that he would die before enjoying even a single night of marital bliss.

I will set aside even this and imagine that the parents approve. At that time, in the "civilized world," women typically brought a dowry with them into marriage, money, jewelry, land, etc. Not so with the people of the North. Brides in Norse culture from ancient times up through the Middle Ages and beyond did not come with a dowery. "The wife does not bring a dower to the husband, but the husband to the wife." This was unheard of in the rest of the known world at that time. In Germania, the bride received valuables from her husband during the marriage ceremony. The groom gifts his bride with "oxen, caparisoned steed, a shield, a spear, and sword at the wedding. By these, the wife is espoused." Live-stock were their most prized possessions, and how wealth was defined. By presenting them to her, it is as if he is giving her a dowery. Those items do not become community property once they are married. They remained hers to pass on to her children and grandchildren. What does the wife give to her husband? Weapons. So, in addition to giving up valuable livestock, the only thing a man gets in return is weapons to continue warring [34].

If a foreigner somehow overcame every hurdle and was able to marry a Norse woman and be accepted into that society, what would his life be like? He would be expected to be a warrior, and his wife and later children would be there on the sidelines of his battles. Tacitus tells us in #8, "Tradition says that armies already wavering and giving way have been rallied by women who, with earnest entreaties and bosoms laid bare, have vividly represented the horrors of captivity, which the Germans fear with such extreme dread on behalf of their women, that the strongest tie by which a state can be bound is the being required to give, among the number of hostages, maidens of noble birth. They even believe that the sex has a certain sanctity and prescience, and they do not despise their counsels, or make light of their answers." In other words, As the Norse fought, their wives and families called to them from just outside the battlefield, reciting the horrors that would await said wives and children if the men failed. The women were highly respected, and the men listened to them. "She comes to her husband as a partner in toils and danger, to suffer and to dare equally with him, in peace and in war... Thus, she is to live; thus, she is to die" [33].

After the wedding, away from the battlefield, what would his day-to-day life be like? Tacitus gives us a glimpse in #20. "In every household, the children, naked and filthy, grow up with those stout frames and limbs which we so much admire. Every mother suckles her own offspring, and never entrusts it to servants and nurses. The master is not distinguished from the slave by being brought up with greater delicacy. Both live amid the same flocks and lie on the same ground..."

For an outsider, daily life would be much harder living amongst the people of the North than it had been prior to moving there, no matter where they came from. On top of that, a man would not be "master" in his own home, at least not in the way the men of Rome perceived it. Once married, the man would be expected to treat his wife as an equal partner. What man, used to the comforts and privileges that wealth provided in the civilized world, would agree to such a menial and unglamorous life in the frozen North? There is no reason to discuss women from the outside wanting to join the people of Germania. No single woman anywhere in the world at that point in time would have had the freedom or ability to move from one household and culture to another. It was, after all, 98 CE.

All things considered, the reason the people of Germania did not intermarry had nothing to do with racism and everything to do with outsiders not wanting to live there. Considering the inhospitable land, lack of riches or items to trade, as well as the absence of the simple comforts found in the "civilized" world, that is totally understandable. What white supremacists have done is take the probable fact that the people of the North did not interbreed and jump to the conclusion that aligned with their ideals, despite there being no evidence to back it up.

If the Old Norse were truly against mixing their blood with foreigners, they never would have taken women captive and brought them home during the Viking Age. In regard to the bloodline, it does not matter whether the women were wives or slaves; children would be produced. Those children would have children. The "pure race" would be diluted. There is no mention that I am aware of anywhere in the myths or stories that even hints at an aversion to mixing with other people.

Time and Evolving Protocols

In Chapter 2, I discussed the importance of looking at things within the context of the time. It is just as important to acknowledge changing customs, beliefs, and norms that happen over time in every culture and religion. When Tacitus wrote Germania, Christianity was a relatively new religion with only about 7,000 followers. Some of them were second or third-generation Christian. If the biblical accounts of Jesus are correct, some of their grandparents or even great-grandparents were present and listened to Jesus preach on various topics. That would only be the case however if the earliest Christian came from a Jewish family [41].

Although I have heard arguments from Christians that the religion today is the same as it was in "Jesus' day," when placed side by side, the life, and beliefs of the earliest Christians are different in many key aspects from the life of Christians today. I could make a list of all the ways in which modern Christians do not mirror the lifestyle that Jesus promoted, but for this argument, the only one that matters is the one regarding who the gospel was meant for.

He said, "I am not sent but unto the lost sheep of the house of Israel" (Matt.15:24). During his life, Jesus told his disciples that his message was only for the Jews. Later, that changed. Jesus made an exception for one woman, but it was Paul who changed the rule for the entire religion. There is nothing, that I am aware of, that points to Jesus, prior to the crucifixion, authorizing that shift in doctrine. I am not bringing this up because I think only Jews should hear about Christianity, just the opposite. The religion changed, it expanded to include others. Why should that be any different for followers of the Norse pantheon?

Even if, originally, Odin and the other Aesir gods were only known to the Old Norse, it should have no bearing on Norse Paganism today. Just as Christianity has spread around the globe, so are there now Norse pagans whose ancestors came from all over the world. For those still clinging to a belief that Norse paganism is only for people of "pure" Germanic or Norse blood, I will turn the discussion away from theology and on to science.

The Truth About Bloodlines

According to an article in Science magazine, "almost all modern humans have this incredibly complex history of mixing and mating and migration." Ever since the discovery of DNA, scientists and archeologists have worked together to trace the migration patterns of people across time. One of the things that they discovered is that "indigenous Europeans" originally came from many different areas including the Middle East. They continued to migrate and mix long after Tacitus wrote his book. The evidence of that can be visually seen in the people themselves. The people of Germania were described as all having blue eyes, red hair, and large stature. Only 3-5% of modern-day Germans have red hair. That fact alone tells us that during the last 2,000 years, descendants of the people written about in Germania migrated to other areas and mixed with different groups of people. There is no "pure" Germanic race [42][43].

Chapter 4
Odin and Thor: The Lessons They Teach Us

Norse paganism is filled with a colorful cast of personalities and deities. Some of the more significant ones include Heimdall, watchman of Asgard, where all the pantheon resides. It also has Freyja, who is the Norse equivalent to Greek's Goddess of Love, Aphrodite. Norse pagans are well versed in all of the names and attributes behind them, but two gods stand out among them all. Even if you are not knowledgeable about Norse culture, you would know the names of the two most popular gods of the Old Norse, Odin (Óðinn, Old Norse) and Thor, (Þór Old Norse). Today and even fifty years ago, their names were being used in comic books and action movies. They are also found on merchandise such as T-shirts, hoodies, mugs, posters, the list goes on and on.

What is so special about these two gods that make them stand out from the rest of the pantheon? The reason is the traits they represent. Thor and Odin not only garnered respect from ancient civilizations but also from people today. Modern Norse pagans look to them for guidance and try to emulate the traits their heroes are famous for. Odin was not typically worshiped by the masses. He was the god of the rulers and society's elite. People today can look to him, as they strive to better themselves and move up in the world. Thor, on the other hand, was the god of the everyday man. He is a god that people can relate to and he in turn understands them and the struggles they are going through.

Unlike in Monotheistic religions, with their one consummate God, the gods are not perfect beings in Norse mythology. They are not treated like you would treat a God in Sunday school. Thor and Odin are no exception. They make mistakes in their respective stories. Both have made rash judgments, lost their temper, and even acted like children in the face of embarrassment. Their emotions and actions are in many ways just like the humans they rule over. This is one of the reasons why Norse paganism calls out to us, so we can relate and learn from them. Despite being powerful enough to do seemingly miraculous things they are still slaves to their very human-like emotions [44].

Odin: A God of Many Names

Odin has over two hundred. Why does one god need so many names? People have long understood that there is power in a name. Some believe that knowing the true name of a demon gives you power over it. Others believe they can cast out demons by invoking their god's name. It is an ancient belief that some religions still hold today. All religions believe that speaking directly to their chosen deity by name draws its attention to you. Monotheistic believers begin prayers by addressing them to their "God." Calling them by name gets God's, or the gods', attention.

Odin is considered, by the majority of Norse pagans, to be the most powerful god in the pantheon. He is also known to lash out at other people on occasion. The ancients probably figured that sometimes getting Odin's attention was not in their best interest. That could be one of the reasons behind some of his names. Instead of talking about him using his given name, they may refer to him by a name that connects him to his family. For example, Baldrsfaðir, "Father of Baldr", Bróðir Vilis, "Brother of Vili", or Frumverr Friggjar, "First Husband of Frigg." There are also plenty of names based on who he regarded as a friend or foe, such as Vinr Míms, "Friend of Mimir," or Bági ulfs, "Enemy of the Wolf."

His physical appearance is also the source of many of his monikers. Several names reference his lack of one eye such as

Bileygr which means Feeble Eye. Others like Hárr and Hoarr translate directly as "One-Eyed." Gestumblindi, meaning "Blind Guest," is not entirely accurate. After all, he still has one eye remaining. His beard and clothing have also inspired a number of his names including Loðungr, "Shaggy Cloak Wearer," Siðgrani, "Longbeard," or simply Karl, "Old Man."

His fierce personality gave rise to some even more names. Hrani, Hrjotr, and Harada translate to "Blusterer, Roarer, and Screamer," respectively. His great wisdom and knowledge provided inspiration. Another of his names, Mjöllnir means very wise it is also the name of Thor's hammer. His personal experiences created a wellspring of pseudonyms such as Ganger or "Wanderer," Runatyr, "God of Runes" and Hangaguð meaning "Hanged God."

Often Odin gave himself alternate names. He was a master of disguise, but any disguise would become useless if he referred to himself as Odin. On his quest to get hold of the Mead of Poetry, he dressed up as a poor farmhand and told people his name was Bolverk. It means simply bale worker, as in one who works with bales of hay.

Finally, his place within the Norse pantheon of gods provides him with one of his most well-known handles, Alfaðir. Most pronounce it today as "All-Father." Overall, there are hundreds, but the most common one is Odin, "Wodan" in old high German. Some scholars believe the name might be the origin of the word "God." For a complete list of Odin's names, check out the "A Special Note" section at the back of the book [44][45].

The Sacrifice for Wisdom

The ancient Vikings believed in the power and wisdom of Odin. For his sake, they put their lives on the line and marched into battle, hoping to get a chance to join his army in Valhalla, Valhöll in Old Norse. Odin is for some heathens the most important deity in their pagan life. His defining trait is wisdom. He is never done learning. The Allfather continuously made sacrifices in order to receive even more knowledge. Through his actions, he teaches us that learning is a lifelong process. No matter where you are or what you are doing, take a moment to identify the things you can learn from that experience.

In many myths, you will see Odin wandering around the different worlds in search of wisdom and more enlightenment. His curiosity ultimately led him to Mimir's well, who was at the time the wisest god of the Norse world. Odin knew that Mimir was drinking the water of this magical well and rightly assumed it was the source of Mimir's enhanced ability to discern. The Allfather asked him to be allowed to drink as well.

Mimir replied that it would cost him a high price in return. To get a swallow of water from this well, on Mimir's demand, he gouged out his eye. This was all done for the sake of wisdom. He then threw his eye into the well. It is unclear how reluctant Odin was. Sacrificing something important can be a tough decision to make, but Odin made that choice, knowing the reward was worth the price. After drinking the water from Mimir's Well he became the wisest of all the gods in Norse mythology [46].

Odin's Ravens: Hugin and Munin

Stories of Odin seeking knowledge are a recurring theme in Norse mythology. Not only did he gouge out his eye, but he went to Hel, became a human sacrifice, and went to the ends of the world to learn more about fate. These are dramatic stories, but Odin had another way to collect information that was not quite as daunting. His two ravens were known to be a source of Odin's insight into earthly events. Their names are Hugin and Munin. The pair flew all over observing human events. Then they returned to Odin to deliver the news of Midgard. In that way, the Allfather was kept abreast of what was going on in the world. They typically report to him at dinner, where they take their place on Odin's shoulders. They are his constant companions.

He does not need the ravens to observe Midgard. He can watch it all from his home in Asgard, but the birds give him a new perspective on what he sees. Odin hung himself on the tree for nine days to learn more about magic and enlightenment. All the while he remained aware of what was taking place across the realms through a steady stream of information from his ravens. They were given their respective names by Odin himself; Hugin meaning thought, and Munin meaning memory. He cares for them very much. A verse in the poetic Edda indicated that he worried that his birds would not return one day. He was stressed about it, especially for Munin. It is a very human emotion to worry that our memory will leave us one day and not return.

The ravens were present long before the writing of the Eddas. Archeologists have found gold plates from the 5th and 6th CE depicting ravens giving guidance to a person on horseback. Odin was often portrayed standing with a spear and having the two ravens on his shoulders. Such depictions have been found all across Europe, probably being distributed by the Vikings that traveled to faraway lands. The ravens were also important in shamanistic rituals, where shamans associated themselves with specific animals, like bears or ravens, to receive the power and abilities the animal possessed. Their imagery and iconography can still be found in different places, across the Viking world [47].

Odin's Origin

Ymir is the first creature and from his body, all beings in Norse mythology originated. So, to discuss Odin's origin, we need to discuss Ymir as well. The creature was a hermaphrodite, meaning he has both male and female parts. In Old Norse, he is also referred to as Aurgelmir, meaning "sand screamer."

Ymir was made after the fire from Muspelheim and ice from Niflheim met in Ginnungagap, which is the abyss of space. While he slept, several giants came into being from his armpits and legs. For food, he got milk from a giant cow named Audhumla. The cow got nourishment by licking a salt rock. Within this rock, was the God Buri. Over time the salt was worn away and Buri was released. He had a son, Borr who started a family with Bestla, a daughter of Ymir. They had three children, Odin, Vili, and Ve [48].

Thor and Odin are father and son, but in many ways, they are the opposites of each other. They tend to banter back and forth. Odin is a god interested in magic, spirituality, wisdom, and war. Thor's main demographic of worshippers were not the elites, but the common man, the hard-working public, which at that time consisted mostly of farmers. Next to his father, the wisest god in Asgard, Thor was often thought of as less than intelligent, "a simpleton." But it is not a fair assessment. His defining traits are his fierceness and bravery in battle, honesty, love of a good time, and willingness to come to the aid of others [49].

Thor and His Myths

After Odin, the most recognizable god is none other than his son, Thor. He is a prominent character in Norse mythology and was a major figure in many Germanic legends before Christianity came and changed the landscape. He became the prevailing deity among warriors, and within the Scandinavian community, his popularity peaked in the late Viking Age. Thor is considered to be more than half-giant. Odin, as mentioned before, is half-giant, and Thor's mother, Jord, the Earthmother, is a full-blooded giant. The giants as a race are not an enemy of the Asgardians, but a few of them are.

Known as the warrior god, a brawny thunder god, with flaming red hair and beard. Thor is the personification of the ideal fighter. Throughout the multitude of stories in the Eddas in which he is a part, his loyalty and honor are on display. The common man or woman is naturally drawn to his charismatic personality. That holds true whether they are alive today or lived thousands of years in the past. He defends the Aesir gods and their home Asgard, and there is no one better suited to the task. The enemies that attack their home base, are typically giants. Thor fights them with his courage and sense of responsibility. In addition, he has immense physical strength and unshakable determination.

Thor carries certain items to help him in his tasks. He has a belt called megingjarðar that makes his strength double whenever he wears it. He also has magical gloves and staff. However, the most recognizable part of his iconography is his hammer, Mjöllnir. Thor's name means thunder, and his hammer translates to lightning. Whenever they saw a storm with heavy thunder and lightning, the people believed an epic battle was happening. Thor was using his hammer to slay the giants while flying across the sky on his goat-drawn chariot.

Thor has an enemy named Jormungand. This creature is a massive sea serpent that completely wraps itself around Midgard with enough remaining length to bite its own tail. In one of the stories, Thor was on a fishing trip. He catches the beast and begins to reel it into the boat. He only stopped after his companion, the giant Hymir, cuts his fishing line out of fear that the serpent, if brought on land, might destroy the world. During Ragnarök, Thor and Jormungand will fight it out and lay each other to rest [49].

Thor the Bride

One of the most popular myths of Thor is when he dressed up as a woman. One day, the God of thunder woke up in horror. He realized that his hammer was missing. He frantically searched everywhere it might possibly be, but he could not find it. So, Thor, along with Loki, went to Freyja to ask for help. She lent them falcon feathers that had the power to shapeshift anyone into a falcon. Then Loki, using the feathers, flew across worlds to find the hammer. He flew to Jötunheim, the world of giants, to investigate. On arrival, he transformed back. Then went to talk with the chief of the giants, Thrym, who confessed that he had the hammer and had buried it underground. The chief had no intention of just handing it over. Surely getting it back was worth a great deal to all the gods. Thrym had a single demand. In exchange for returning Thor's hammer, the Goddess of Love, Freyja, had to marry him.

When Loki returned with the news. The gods were angry, and the angriest among them was Freyja. As the discussion ended, Heimdall suggested sending Thor to Jötunheim dressed as Freyja. The gods all thought it was a good idea. He could take back the hammer and destroy his enemies then and there. Thor fought back against the plan, saying that it was unbecoming of a man to dress as a woman. However, Loki told him that it was an easy task that could save Asgard and prevent it from falling into the giant's hands. Thor finally agreed. His gown was crafted beautifully. Loki was dressed as the "bride's" maidservant. Together they went to Jötunheim.

Thrym was very happy to see them, but Thor almost gave himself away at dinner. He consumed an entire ox, salmon, various dainties, and many barrels of mead. Thrym was confused at the sight of a woman with such an enormous appetite. Thinking quickly, Loki explained that the fair goddess had been so lovesick that she could not bring herself to eat for an entire week. Later, when the giant went to kiss his bride, he commented on Thor's frightening eyes. Loki then deceitfully said that the goddess had not only been unable to eat, but sleep had precluded her as well.

The party continued, and Thrym took out the hammer to hollow the wedding. As soon as he placed it in his bride's eager hands, all pretense disappeared. Thor swung his hammer. Soon all the giants present, including Thrym, was slain [50].

Sif's Hair and Thor's Hammer

What does his wife's hair have to do with Thor's iconic weapon? The hammer Mjöllnir is the most recognizable item in Thor's inventory. The weapon's origin has an elaborate myth of its own. Loki, the God of trickery and deceit, was at times Thor's sidekick as in the story just told. Thor's wife, Sif was a beautiful fertility goddess. The Jötunn (giants), and even many of the gods, were more than a little jealous of Thor for having such a gorgeous bride, with her long golden hair. Hanging out with her husband, Loki saw Sif on a regular basis. As he watched her and listened to the comments of others, the gears in his mischief-seeking brain began to turn. One important thing to know about Loki is that he rarely stops to think about the consequences of his actions before he takes them.

One night, while Thor was away, Loki crept into their room and found the fair Sif fast asleep. There is no record of why Loki decided to do what he did next, perhaps he went there with the intent, or just as likely, it was a fleeting impulse. It doesn't matter because the result was the same. Loki cut off her exquisite hair. When Sif woke the next morning she was overcome with distress. Word of the event soon reached Thor. He knew immediately that the culprit was none other than his fair-weather friend, Loki. In a rage, he confronted the trickster, threatening to break every bone in his body. To save himself, Loki promised to make things right by enlisting the help of some dwarves. The dwarves were known for their superior craftsmanship. Thor finally agreed to forestall the beating when Loki assured him that Sif's replacement hair would be made with pure gold [51][52].

Before the angry husband could change his mind, Loki set out for Svartalfheim, the realm of the dwarfs. He approached a group of dwarves, the sons of Ivaldi, and asked if they were able to produce such an item. Being great craftsmen, they soon agreed to make Sif's golden hair. When they were done, they presented to Loki, not one but three gifts for the gods. The first was a wig of spun gold that when placed on Sif's head would attach and grow as if it were real hair. The second gift was a magical ship for the fertility god Freyr, named Skíðblaðnir, which could fly in the air as easily as it sailed on water. It was massive, big enough to hold all of the gods yet when folded, small enough to fit in his pocket. The third gift was Gungnir, Odin's famous spear that never missed its mark.

Loki returned to Asgard and began to rave about how great the gifts were that he planned to give the gods, proclaimed that they were the finest of dwarf creations. He went on to boast that no one could make items of finer quality. Standing nearby was a visitor from Svartalfheim, the dwarf Brokk. No sooner had Loki paused to take a breath, when Brokk angrily interjected, "My brother, Eitri and I can create gifts for the gods every bit as good, or even better than the sons of Ivaldi."

Unhappy at losing the spotlight, Loki quickly countered, "I will bet my head against yours, that you and your brother cannot make three other treasures equally as good." Brokk accepted the wager and soon left for home. He was eager to tell his brother about the bet and begin work on the valuable offerings [53].

Eitri prepared a pigskin and placed it in the furnace. Brokk's job was to work the bellows. "Do not pause for even a moment, brother. Keep the air flowing to the fire until I return and take the skin out myself." Eitri then left, as Brokk continued to pump the bellows. Unbeknownst to either of them, Loki had followed Brokk back to the family's smithy. Never one to worry about fair play, Loki transformed himself into a fly and began buzzing around the dwarf. The god-turned-fly landed on his hand and stung him painfully, but Brokk never slowed. Soon, Eitri returned and removed his work from the furnace. What went in as a lifeless pigskin came out as a magnificent boar with golden bristles.

Next, he put in some gold and again instructed his brother to work the bellow and not stop until he returned. Eitri left and the fly again started to torment Brokk. It buzzed all around him, flying higher this time, around the dwarf's shoulders, before finally landing on his neck. This time the sting was even worse than the first. Still, the bellow was worked, without interruption, until Eitri reappeared and retrieved the gold. It had been transformed into the gold ring, Draupnir.

Lastly, Eitri put iron inside the furnace, admonishing his brother to work the bellows without a pause. This time he added a warning, "otherwise all would be worthless." Then he again left. Loki the fly was beginning to panic, after all, his head was on the line. He took to the air and began buzzing all around the dwarf's head, darting in and out, a constant irritating torment. Brokk continued his work, with never a break in the flow of air. Then the fly landed right between his eyes. It stung him fiercely until blood poured down and he could no longer see. Finally, he paused to smack the fly away. The bellows stopped only for a moment. His brother came back into the smithy and ranted at him, "all that lay in the furnace came near being entirely spoiled." He then removed the final object. It was the hammer, Mjöllnir.

During the ruckus, Loki returned to his normal state, then silently stood at the door looking on. Eitri grabbed all three creations and handed them to Brokk. The trickster made his presence known. Eitri then enjoined his brother to go with Loki back to the home of the gods, without a glance towards the mischief-making god, he added "fetch the wager," and all standing there knew that he spoke of Loki's head.

In almost every image of Thor, you will see Mjöllnir in his hands. It has a unique ability. Long before Western civilization knew such a thing existed, Thor's hammer acted like a boomerang. Even better than that, it was, and is, a boomerang with the abilities of a guided missile. When he throws his hammer, it goes straight to the target, striking his opponent, and then soars safely back into Thor's waiting hand. It is said that the hammer has never missed its target. The hammer must be wielded with special gloves. The gloves, hammer, and belt are always his companions in battles. But Mjöllnir is not perfect. Thanks to Loki's meddling, it came out of the furnace with too short of a handle.

How was the wager between Brokk and Loki decided? In case you are wondering, I will finish the story. Once back in Asgard, all the gods sat up high on their "doom-steads" and looked on as Loki handed out the creations made by the sons of Ivaldi. He gave the spear, Gungnir to Odin. To Thor, he handed Sif's hair of spun gold. Then he gave the last gift to Freyr, the magical ship, Skíðblaðnir.

Next, it was Brokk's turn to pass out gifts. He gave Odin the ring and explained that every ninth night, eight more identical rings would appear and drop from the first. He then went to Freyr and gifted him the boar, telling him that it could sprint faster than any horse, except Odin's. The boar had the ability to run anywhere, including the sea and sky. Day or night it could travel because of the golden bristles which would light up the dark. Finally, he came to Thor. Brokk handed him the special hammer. All the gods listened on as the dwarf described its abilities. Mjöllnir is indestructible. No matter what he hit with the hammer, it would never break. It also should never be lost because the weapon returns to its owner whenever thrown. If Thor ever needed to conceal it, Mjöllnir can shrink small enough to fit under his clothes and not be seen. Brokk then admitted its single flaw. The handle is shorter than they meant it to be.

Since all of the gifts went to Odin, Freyr, or Thor, it was decided that they alone would determine the outcome of the wager. They all agreed that despite its flaw, Thor's hammer was the best treasure and the greatest protector. What happened next, between Brokk and Loki, is another story. If you are curious, you can read how it all ends in Skáldskaparmál, from Snorri Sturluson's Prose Edda [53].

The hammer is not perfect, but Thor's usage and full utilization of its capabilities made it so. The thunder god accepted the flaw in the hammer and never used it as an excuse for failure in battle. He did not lower his expectations of himself or his weapon because something was wrong with it. He adapted, learning how to adjust his handgrip and throw, and in doing so, overcame its shortcomings [54].

We can learn a lot from Thor. When things are less than ideal and obstacles slow you down, think of Thor's hammer. It serves as an analogy for all of the less-than-perfect items and events that we must work with and through if we want to live our best lives. It is important not to wait until things are perfect or ideal before taking the next step in your personal journey. Things, including timing, are rarely perfect, but just look at what Thor is able to do with his imperfect hammer.

I heard something recently that does not pertain to Norse paganism directly, but it fits well here. I rarely watch television, but I saw a clip from an episode of American's Got Talent online. A tiny wisp of a woman walked out on stage. She and the judges chatted for a moment, and she nonchalantly let it slip, that she was terminally ill. The judges were flabbergasted that she was even there. What she said next stuck with me. "You can't wait until life isn't hard anymore before you decide to be happy. Her name is Jane Marczewski. She then sang a song she wrote herself called "It's Okay," for which she received a standing ovation [55].

Her heartfelt statement should be a fill-in-the-blank mantra for us all. "You can't wait until (blank) before you (blank)."

For some, it might be, "You can't wait until your workload lightens before you go back to school." For others, it might be, "You can't wait until retirement before you take a vacation." For Thor, it would be, "You can't wait until you have a perfect weapon before you fight the enemies of Asgard." For too many people, what they are waiting for never happens. As a result, neither do their dreams.

Some Thoughts on Loki

There is an aspect of Loki which has in modern times made him a deity worthy of worship. That is as a god of the transgender community. I am not aware of any literature that addresses this issue, but it is worth discussing. My awareness of this aspect of Loki's adoration is based on the views of those I know and care about within the trans community. Throughout history, transgender people have been forced to hide who they really are, out of a very real threat to their health, livelihood, even their life. Most are never able to live their lives to the fullest, as their authentic selves. Things are getting better. We now have gay marriage and anti-discrimination laws that protect same-sex couples. Few people still feel the need to remain "in the closet," out of fear for their personal safety or out of concern that being "out" would make life much more difficult.

There are still too many homophobic people and religious institutions that promote hate, but it has gotten far better. Western society has long cast transgender people as outside the accepted norm. Due to public demonstrations and LGBTQ-backed media campaigns the plight of the transgender community has recently come to the forefront. That does not mean that the discrimination and violence against them have gotten better.

Most people turn to the government and governmental agencies when they are attacked or discriminated against. For the transgender community, the government from local police to state governors is part of the problem. Loki is a god they can relate to. In addition to his penchant for wearing dresses and mocking the rules of society, he is an outsider even within the ranks of his own people, the Norse Gods [56][57].

For Norse Pagans, choosing which god or gods to worship is a very personal choice. For some members of the trans community choosing Loki is a logical choice, despite the fact that there is no known evidence that he was personally worshiped during the time of the Vikings.

Chapter 5
The Metamorphosis of Old Norse Culture

Whistle hen you think of Vikings, what image comes to mind? Do you picture hordes of terrifying heathens, swarming a defenseless monastery, stealing the church's gold and religious artifacts? Perhaps you think of them as explorers, highly skilled sailors, able to navigate their shallow boats over the open ocean, to discover new lands. Or you might think of them as maritime opportunists, able to traverse hundreds of miles upriver in order to plunder wealthy cities like Paris? Maybe you have a more pastoral view. One in which they lived as farmers at home and later set up farming communities in England, just wanting to live a peaceful life. It may be that you envision mercenaries, paid by foreign governments to fight in distant lands. All of these images are correct, but none is complete. What most people will agree on though is that once the Vikings became Christian, it was the end of those Viking ways. On that point, they would be wrong.

Vikings Across Europe

No one knows why in 787, Norsemen left their homes for foreign lands. It may be that they were on a quest to find better land to settle and farm. It could also be that those first ships were sent out as scouts to find the best place to launch an initial attack. All we know for sure is that they returned in mass three years later. They landed on the shores of Northumbria and attacked the monastery in Lindisfarne. By the time they climbed back into their unique boats, the place had been emptied of all its valuables. The interior was utterly decimated along with priceless, irreplaceable books and holy relics. Anyone who got in their way, including monks and nuns, was cut down. The Viking Age had begun.

Christians were initially stunned. God was too powerful. They believed that their churches, convents, monasteries, and other religious properties were under God's protection. No heathen should be mighty enough to cause such destruction. The only way they could come to terms with it was to believe that for some reason God allowed it to happen as punishment for sin. The local Christian community prayed for forgiveness. It became a time of deep introspection and renewed commitments to piety across the Christian world. What the masses did not understand was that the attack had nothing to do with religion. The Vikings attacked churches for two reasons. They contained lots of wealth and they were poorly defended [58].

The Christians viewed the heathens not as a separate people with their own lives and history, but a chapter of their history and how they were a trial sent from God. They wrote about the events in their religious contexts. It was very hard on the Christians when they saw Vikings beat them at numerous battles and their God not helping them, even if they fasted and prayed. The Vikings believed in fate, so they did not have a catastrophic reaction from losses.

Over the next hundred years, the Vikings struck further and further from home. They attacked coastal areas around England, Ireland, and Scotland. Often attacking the same place over and over again. They raided Islands and port towns from Northern France, around the coast of Portugal and Spain, and into the Mediterranean Sea. There they struck Italy, Sicily, and North Africa. Due to their boats' unique ability to traverse both oceans and rivers in the same vessel, they were also able to reach rich cities in the heart of Europe including Paris and Hamburg. They made it into parts of Eastern Europe all the way to the edges of Western Asia. Longboats filled with warriors traveled down through modern-day Russia to the Black and Caspian Seas. They went as far south and east as Constantinople [59].

For many decades the Norsemen were free to perpetuate the carnage. No one could stop them. Starting in the mid-9th century, instead of returning home after raids they set up camps and wintered in places with a better climate than Scandinavia.

Their raids did more than just supply wealth. They exposed the Old Norse to things they could not have imagined. The biggest of which was a new religion, Christianity. Prior to that, there was no name for the collective beliefs of the Norse people. Their myths and lore provided a lens through which they viewed the world. Only after the new religion arrived, did the people need a word to identify the sum total of their beliefs: about the world around them, how it was created, the various beings that inhabited it, as well as the culture and traditions that had been passed down to them for a thousand years or more. They referred to it as Forn Siðr. Which translates to "old customs" [59].

Norse pagan beliefs were similar to other pre-Christian belief systems, such as the ancient Greek or Romans. They all had many gods with vibrant social lives. Like the Norse pantheon, Greek and Roman gods got married and had children. They also had unique personalities with human-like flaws and emotions. The behavior and values of each pantheon of gods reflected the society in which their followers lived. The Old Norse ideology and rituals were fully integrated into Scandinavian society. Today, we call it a religion, but it was truly a way of life. A habit of doing things and thinking in a certain way that applied to their daily routines. Paganism became known as a religion only after Christianity settled in Europe.

Christianity Arrives in Scandinavia

During the year 725, Christian priests arrived on the shores of Scandinavia. They went there with the hope of converting the region. Among them was Willibrord of Utrecht, later known as Saint Willibrord, an Anglo-Saxon, who led a mission into Denmark. The locals were not hostile to the priests. In the early 9th century, Christian missionaries started to land on Viking soil, and they too were allowed to be there in peace. The missionaries were numerous, but they could not cross the language barrier to reach the hearts of the local people. As a result, the missionaries did not convert many of them to Christianity.

Over time, in some areas, small groups of newly baptized Christians and local pagans lived peacefully as neighbors. Archeological evidence there, reveals that religious items specific to the two belief systems were sold in local markets. When you traveled to one of their shops, you could easily find Christian crosses and Thor's hammer, both hanging on the same walls. The ancient pagans did not discriminate against the newly converted Christians in their area. They held little or no animosity towards the former-pagan converts. Historians believe this was in part because the converts did not fully understand the new religion. That misunderstanding was not by accident [60].

During 950, Håkon the Good came to Scandinavia attempting to use his authority to establish Christianity and increase his standing as a royal. However, this mission was a failure. The local chieftains refused to work with him. The chieftains in Norse pagan culture were both the legal/political leaders and the religious leaders of their respective communities. Scholars say the shift from paganism to Christianity was slow and gradual. Groups in Scandinavia changed religions when their local chieftains converted and were baptized. Most locals did not convert based on their own personal convictions.

Then came Olav Tryggvason, the former king of Norway who dramatically sped up Christianity's spread. When he came back to reclaim his throne in 995, he arrived with a ship full of priests. On the island of Moster, he held the first Christian mass. In three decades, Christianity became the official religion of the region. It was not the same Christianity however that was practiced by the rest of Europe [60].

Norway has ancient stave churches which clearly show the mixing of Christianity and Viking symbols. These churches were built until the twelfth century. The churches have dragon and portal carvings that tell the story of Norse mythology. The Romanesque basilica-style churches are carved with both Norse and Christian-influenced designs. The mixing could also be seen in cemeteries. The ancient Scandinavians were buried with hammers or crosses in these cemeteries together.

Another example can be seen when you look at Viking coins from the UK. During the Viking era, the coins had the name 'Saint Peter.' The coin's mark of 'PETRI', if closely inspected, would reveal a hammer in the place of the letter 'I.' This is most likely Thor's hammer [60].

Meanwhile in the British Isles...

Beginning in the 860s, they set up permanent settlements on the British Isles and in France. This meant they had to change their ways, at least in those areas. It was imperative they become decent neighbors, or the local inhabitants would have been forced to flee the settled areas, leaving the new immigrants without a reliable source of knowledge about farming in the area. It would also mean they had no one from which to get needed supplies until their own crops came in. They began to trade, to do business with the people in other countries. The church was not supportive of that turn of events.

Local officials and the church wanted the raids to stop, but they soon discovered that doing business with heathens in one area did not preclude Viking carnage in another. As a result, there was no incentive on the part of religious leaders to compromise. The church put out a proclamation. Christians were only to do business with other Christians. Of course, Christians continued to trade with people from Asia and the Middle East without imposing the same requirement. Many Vikings underwent temporary baptism or agreed to "prim-signing" or "first-signing" to show the intent to be baptized at a later date so that they could trade with Christians. They were open to the idea in large part because they did not understand the new religion. Ancient Vikings believed in numerous gods, accepting one more would not have been difficult for them. The early Norse Christians believed in a polytheistic version of Christianity. Norse mythology encourages diversity and acceptance of other beings and other people. There is no way to predict how they would have reacted to the situation if they truly understood the church's ultimate goal to rid the religion of the old gods entirely.

The Tide Begins to Turn

The Christians lost battles continuously for a century. Local priests and monks were frustrated that their leaders were unable to protect them. Early on, the reaction to the raids was for people to pray and supplicate to God. It did not help. The Vikings respected strength and courage. They had contempt for men who begged for mercy instead of fighting back. Neither side understood the other's perspective. The Norse had no concept of sin. Even without a language barrier, they could not be appealed to using a moral argument.

Many men in the church were younger sons of noblemen. The laws and traditions at that time favored the oldest son. They were the only ones to inherit titles and estates. The younger sons needed a different way to survive. Working for someone else or supporting themselves with a common trade was considered beneath them. Society was very class structured. It left few options for second or third sons. Often a nobleman would give a large donation to a religious order at the time their sons reached adulthood. The young men would then join that order. Being raised on a noble estate meant that part of their education was military-type training, riding horses, and fighting with swords.

It was these younger sons, in the church, that finally turned the tide. Realizing no one was going to save them, they took up arms and began to fight back. The leaders in the church were dumbfounded with losses and continued to wring their hands until the noble monks and clergy, using their military training, went into battle themselves. Bishop Heahmund of Wessex was one such person. They commanded armies and brought victories to Christian Europe, with the church firmly behind them. The king's armies also started to win. This changed the Viking's views on the Christian God. When Christendom won, they forced the Viking warriors to convert to Christianity and insisted the heathens be baptized. Many Norse warriors were repeatedly baptized as a result. Most did not take it seriously, but some turned it to their advantage. Viking leaders, such as Olav, Harald Gormsson, Magnus the Good, and several others, changed their religion to ally with the Christians. As a result, many received land and even great riches.

Another reason for the spread of the new religion was that the Vikings were avid slave catchers and traders. In order to facilitate that business, they intermixed with people from far away, most of whom held drastically different views from their own. This included Christianity. In 'Erik the Red's Saga,' the main character Leif Erikson converts his mother to Christianity, and she then tries to convert her husband as well. Most of the time, these heterogeneous religious homes were harmonious, but as with families everywhere throughout history, sometimes they were not.

The most profound change came when the Vikings tried to attack "the Great City," Constantinople. It was the first time they faced an army at sea they could not conquer. They were in awe of the huge city with its great infrastructure, wealth, and splendor. The Byzantine Emperor was likewise impressed with their fighting prowess. He created the Varangian Guard, a group of elite Norse fighters. Each would fight on behalf of the emperor for four years and then return to Scandinavia with wealth and stories of the opulent city. In order to join the Varangians, the warriors had to become Christians. So, they started to convert in order to become part of that beautiful city. The Vikings began to think of the Christian God as a war god and gained respect for the religion [61].

For the vast majority of Norse communities, the people converted to the new faith because their leader converted. The local leaders learned that there was a great deal that could be gained by joining the religion. They gained legitimacy and support from the church and other European rulers. Those who did not convert lost land and power. These top-to-down and bottom-to-top conversions all helped the spread of Christianity. While many think that converting to the new religion would make the Vikings different, the first converts never truly changed their views on how to live a good life. They loved war and battles, some had multiple wives. They had slaves and blood-battles between themselves. These early Christians were

still influenced by their pagan upbringing. It took a few generations before they were true Christians in belief and actions.

Many Norse pagans did not realize the depth and seriousness
of the differences between the faiths. For them, the Christian
God was just one more god. There had always been other
cultures, with their own gods and the Vikings were aware of
that. The newest god though had to have been impressive for
people who lived with the fickleness of some of the Norse
deities. The Christian God did not fit the mold of the gods
they knew. He was above the flaws of human emotion.
Initially, there was little conflict within their beliefs between
worshiping just the gods in the Norse pantheon and
worshiping the old gods along with the newer, all-powerful
Christian God [61].

How Christianity Took Hold in Scandinavia

"The Norse were partially Christian before the formal
conversion began, and they remained partially pagan long
after it had been officially completed." The conversion of
Scandinavian countries was not war-like but, for the most
part, peaceful, slow, and welcoming. When Vikings started to
raid the Christian countries of Britain, Ireland, and Scotland,
they adapted to their local culture and sometimes incorporated aspects of them into daily lives. One of the first Norse

settlers in Iceland was Helgi the Lean. He was baptized and reported himself as Christian, but he still called upon Thor for help and protection in times of need. When this man came to Iceland, he named his settlement "Kristsnes" meaning Christ's Headland [62].

Christianity has a strict set of beliefs and practices. However, many Norse men and women did not adopt them as a whole, instead, they picked them up gradually one by one. This process of conversion took centuries. Full conversion came when people started to forget their old pagan practices, not when Christianity was first introduced. This happened during the eleventh and twelfth centuries. Every country, locality, or province has its history of missionaries, missions, and conversion stories.

The first attempt at converting the Danes was by the Franks at the hands of Charlemagne. He acquired land south of Denmark and violently acted to change the region's religion but was largely unsuccessful. History tells us that the conversion of the people to Christianity was mainly by the hands of a man named Ansgar. He was the Archbishop of Hamburg-Bremen. First, this German priest contacted and successfully converted the king of Denmark. Later on, he also built churches and monasteries. The Franks sent missionaries as well and built a few churches. However, the real change came to the people of Denmark when the first proper king Harald

Gormsson, also known as Harald Bluetooth, converted to Christianity.

In Norway, the people were much more willing to accept Christianity and even had a bishop after the year 960. The chieftains were the local leaders, and the King of Norway at the time was the only person who owned large amounts of land. King Håkon Aðalsteinsfostri, the youngest son of King Harald Fairhair of Norway, was raised in England as the foster-son of the Anglo-Saxon king, Æþelstan. While there, he was converted to Christianity and baptized. After King Harald died, his favorite son, Erik Bloodaxe became king. The son was a tyrant and very unpopular. With the backing of the Anglo-Saxon king, Håkon conquered his older half-brother and was crown King Håkon the Good. He established much of the church structure in the country but did not push his people to convert.

It was after Håkon the Good's death, and a period with no king, that King Olav appeared and pushed to spread Christianity as a way to showcase his power. He conquered the entire country. He was a Viking leader that raided English lands. After several victories, the English bribed him with money and support so that he would leave them alone. By using that money, political support from England, and the new faith, he ruled Norway and insisted his countrymen accept Christianity.

Iceland was different. It was an island that was founded after the intermixing of Vikings and Christians, so Christianity was always a part of daily life, even if it was not very defined. Full conversion started when Olav sent a German priest to Iceland. He managed to convert some people but also killed a few that retaliated against him. When Olav heard about this, he threatened to kill the Icelanders in Norway.

To avoid bloodshed, two Christian Icelanders named Gizurr the White and Hjalti Skeggjason went to resolve the issue. Their demands were met on the condition that the entire island was converted. Iceland's center of law and government was an assembly, the Alþingi. The decision on which religion would survive was decided there. The people were deeply divided on the topic. However, in the end, Christianity was adopted as the national faith. Paganism was allowed to be practiced privately, but everyone on the island needed to be baptized.

Sweden took a long time to convert to Christianity, but by the 12th century, the country had forgotten paganism. Different kings came and became Christians themselves, and a section of people would convert each time. This happened until King Anund, who ruled in 1022, came, and almost all of Sweden converted.

For Greenland's conversion, we can look to the Saga of Erik the Red. Leif Eriksson was converted by Olav, and he later converted his mother and father Erik. His famous story is about a Viking changing his faith to Christianity. There is a small church in Brattahlid built called Erik's settlement. Not much is known about their conversion, but Adam of Bremen wrote in 1070 that the region turned to Christianity [62].

What Happened to The Old Faith?

As time went on, only the relics and symbols of paganism were left. The highly regarded pagan festival of Yuletide that celebrated the rise of the sun was blended into the Christian holiday we all know as Christmas. However, it is fascinating to note that the Scandinavian countries still refer to this holiday as "Jul."

The church added new practices in order to incorporate some aspects of pagan beliefs that the locals clung to. For example, in Norse mythology, each farmland had a protector spirit or sprite called a Nisse or Tomte in Danish and Norwegian, respectively. They are tiny creatures that resemble Santa's elves in appearance. Special bowls of porridge with butter on top, called julegrøt, are left out for them every Christmas Eve. It is a practice that continues in Scandinavian countries to this day. These compromises were important because they helped the Norse pagans slide into Christianity and accept it without detailed knowledge of the religion. It was a way to convert them [63].

The Demonization of Norse Paganism

Demonization was a strategy that the Church used to delegitimize different religions, not just Norse paganism. It is a way to reinterpret and represent polytheistic religions and their gods as evil, run by Satan and his demons. The need for demonization shows that many people still practiced paganism during medieval times. To further their hold on Scandinavian countries, collect the tax, control the people, and retain power within the church, the non-conforming people needed to be subjugated. Thus, pagan worship began being associated with evil. The diverse cast of Norse mythology, along with their qualities and powers, began to be called devilish. Loki has shapeshifting powers and demonstrated gender fluidity, which later became satanic-like qualities.

Norse gods were a source of guidance and protection. They were not viewed as wicked before Christianity came to Scandinavia. Gods were beings that regulated the functions of earth and looked after the people. There were gods associated with different events, elements of nature, and places. Odin was a god of wisdom and battles. Thor was a God of thunder and warriors. The god Freyr and goddess Freya were the gods of fertility and the harvest. They were not perfect, but neither was anything else in the Norse world. Odin was not above using deceit, and Thor was quick to anger. Each of them showed important human characteristics, such as loyalty, honor, wisdom, and strength in larger-than-life ways. They represented nature, with both nurturing and destructive characteristics. Going into battle and being carried by the Valkyries, the Norse mythology glorified not just life, but also death. These beliefs gave a sense of hope to a chaotic life [64].

The church did not want the people to focus on the conditions and circumstances of their life. The leaders of the church could not make those things better any more than the Norse gods could. Instead, of finding meaning and purpose during their lifetime, the church sold people on the idea of a better afterlife in heaven. It also introduced the ideas of sin and eternal punishment. It was and continues to be an ideal way to control the masses. Promise them something that cannot be proven. Get them to believe that focusing on bettering themselves and acquiring great things in this life is bad, while at the same time, wanting a wonderful life for eternity is good and noble. Then dictate everything required of them to attain that desired afterlife.

From Power to Subservience

The changing role of women in Norse society as a result of Christianity meant they went from a place of power, where a woman was valued for her strength and resourcefulness and looked to for her "magic" abilities, to a place of subservience. With Christianity firmly in control, traditional women and women's roles in Old Norse society were demonized. Cut-out witches on brooms with black cats are familiar decorations for Halloween. That image comes from the völva, which were Old Norse women considered to have "magical powers." Like Freyja, whose chariot was pulled by cats, many völva had cat companions. These typically older women of Scandinavia worked in the healing arts or divination. The church declared that they were witches, a term from the bible already associated with evil. As a result, all the things they were known for doing fell under the definition of witchcraft. The campaign to erase the strong women of the North began with the demonization of these women.

The Middle Ages were a time in which "witchcraft," including the natural healing methods used by these women, was seen as a crime comparable to murder. The advent of Christianity changed people's views on magic and witchcraft. On the one hand, what they did was referred to as superstitious nonsense. On the other hand, there was never-ending persecution of witches because they were considered to be so dangerous. In order to remove pagan influence, laws were enacted, and religious leaders gave speeches about how witchcraft was related to the devil, and people associated with it needed to be "cleansed by fire." One of the proponents of this line of thought was Saint Augustine.

Rumors about the powers of pagan women sorcerers were spread. Some of the most common beliefs were that they had demons under control, had sexual relations with demons, and were using magic to trick or force other people into doing their bidding. The negative magical spells were known as curses, and these women were believed to be using them for harmful purposes. Positive spells were enchantments that were meant to help the one requesting them. From the twelfth to the thirteenth century, people had divided opinions about witchcraft and magic. At one end, there were healers, and on the other, there were evil sorcerers. The women practicing the first would be called white or wise witches and the other, black witches. The law did not differentiate between the two kinds.

If someone was accused of being a witch, then that person was labeled a heretic and was dealt with. The person could have been a man or woman, but it was mostly women who were accused of these so-called crimes. The punishment for the crime was typically hanging. Women were not burned at the stake for being a witch during medieval times. That punishment did not start until the sixteenth century, hundreds of years after the Viking Age [65].

Women in the Old Norse culture were not given every right that a man had, but they were much better off than women in other cultures and religions around the world at that time. Historians like to point out "the exception to the rule," women who had more autonomy, personal wealth, or privilege. Those exceptions were rare, and to focus on far less than 1% of women, does not give an accurate picture of what life was like for the vast majority of Christian women in the Middle Ages.

The scars left by history are still present today. Until relatively modern times women did not enjoy equal rights or protection under the law. Businesses could legally discriminate against women in a broad range of ways from denying a woman credit without a male co-signer, to single women not being allowed to enter bars alone. Laws have been corrected, but religious people follow two sets of rules, laws of the land and God's laws. Those "rules" prescribed by monotheistic religions continue to place women beneath men in substantial ways.

Chapter 6
Magic in Norse Paganism

People, since the beginning of civilization, searched for ways to help heal the sick and injured. They did whatever they could think of to make their crops grow and keep their animals healthy. When those things went wrong, survival was precarious. Modern science has created medicines that can reduce fevers, heal infections, and even stop the progression of some diseases. Science has revolutionized farming. Technology continues to change the world. None of that was available to those people.

The modern image of magic in ancient or medieval times is somewhat distorted. Medieval magic is still often portrayed as it was by Shakespeare in Macbeth, "Double, double toil and trouble; Fire burn and cauldron bubble," the three witches chanted while dropping in disgusting ingredients like "Eye of newt and toe of frog, wool of bat and tongue of dog." There are also plenty of skewed examples involving Sorcerers. Most people have seen at least a clip of Mickey Mouse as the hapless assistant in the Sorcerer's Apprentice. The sorcerer had total command of inanimate objects, but his most impressive feat was his ability to control nature itself. This imagery is not in historically accurate. Scholars have seldom found any evidence of even attempts at such practices, whether it be in medieval literature or historical records from that time. There are some examples, but such elaborate attempts were a rare occurrence rather than the norm [66][67].

Magic in the Middle Ages

There are two ways to interpret magic in this era, everyday magic, which encompassed the daily lives of the masses, and magic in medieval literature which was not common and only done by specific people. Everyday magic allowed the common man to believe she or he could do things outside the bounds of human capability. It consisted of superstitions, actions that included chanting of spells and performing rituals, and ideas that governed people's thinking. Words and actions were used together to solve certain problems that at the time were otherwise unsolvable.

In the last chapter, I discussed how magic within Norse Pagan society got a bad reputation with the spread of Christianity and false claims by the church. However, magic was an everyday occurrence across Europe in medieval times. The practice of it was not confined to the Old Norse. It was a normal part of daily life for the average person. It is important to remember that prior to Christianity, all of Europe held some version of pagan beliefs. As areas became Christian, the people would carry over the parts of their old culture that did not have a comparable component in the new religion. "The boundary between paganism and Christianity was more fluid than it is today" [68].

It is not difficult to understand their desperation. Today, we enjoy technology, scientific discoveries, and an abundance of layered knowledge that led to important inventions and solutions to the majority of problems people face. A person in medieval times, knowing nothing about accurate science or medicine, having no social programs to fall back on in times of crisis, turned to magic to give them hope in their sometimes hopeless situations. It served a purpose. Magic gave them a sense of power and control over an unpredictable and terrifying world.

Everyday magic was not flashy or gory like old playwrights or modern media portrays it to be. It consisted of superstitious words and actions, but it was meaningful to society. Before the twelfth century, authorities and the church did not have a problem with magic. People were not condemned for it. It was not confined to a specific class of people; everyone did it.

If it were only practiced by illiterate peasants, the many books written on the topic at that time would have served no purpose.

Examples of everyday magic are abundant. Most books concerning the topic in this period were about healing. It was the most used, most popular, and most accepted form of magic. There were recipes to get rid of sickness and others to heal an injury. You could also find instructions on how to heal common ailments in different types of animals. An old English Leechbook described how some practices went. The reader was given steps to make medicine using edible plants. Then, to heighten the potency, they had to say certain words and call upon a god for their help; it could have been a pagan deity or the Christian God. For example, if a woman was past due to give birth, she was advised to step on a grave three times and say some specific charms. Sometimes they would need to draw a symbol next to the patient for the added blessing of their god.

People also used magic for protection, from both humans and evil supernatural beings. In the Leechbook, there is a recipe for a drink to remove evil spirits. The ingredients included a piece of paper in which a prayer was traced and was washed by a virgin under running water. This, with some herbs and concentrated wine mixed with water, made the drink. Another form of protection magic used amulets. They were physical objects that needed to be carried or specifically placed to protect you. It could be a picture of a saint, a pouch of herbs, some kind of rock, and even leftover bread. It is where the idea of carrying a rabbit's foot for luck comes from [69].

Peasants in the Middle Ages were not literate, but they did not need to be able to read the Leechbook in order to learn what to do. The information "circulated in folk or peasant cultures and took many shapes and served many purposes." The charms and incantations were also passed down from generation to generation.

The farmer, to protect his crops from failure or the bad effects of a curse, needed to do an elaborate and time-consuming ritual. It went like this. "*Before dawn, cut four pieces of turf from the four sides of the field. Then, mix together oil, honey, yeast, milk from each... cattle, a piece of every tree... a piece of every kind of plant (except buck-bean), and holy water. Drip some of the mixture on each side of the turf while repeating a Latin blessing.*" You are not done yet though. "*Next, head to church... get the priest to sing four masses over the turf... before the sun sets, take the turf back to where you got it. Then carve sayings into four pieces of 'Christ's flour'... Put those in the holes. Then, put the turf carefully back on top.*"

The poor farmer still had a long way to go. The number nine must have held significance because next, he had to bow nine times, and with each bow recite a lengthy Latin prayer nine times, then *"Turn three times towards the sun, stretch out along the ground, and count your litanies there..."* And more prayers to, *"Christ and to holy Mary and to the Holy Rood in praise and worship."* The poor farmer is now about halfway done but he still needs to find a well-fed beggar, drill some trees, recite a lot more Latin, bake holy water in lots of bread, do some plowing, and finally, more Latin *"Crescite... benedicti. Amen."* Amen! There was no guarantee of success but going to such elaborate ends shows how desperate the people in the Middle Ages were to protect their crops. Starvation was a real possibility [70].

In addition to common magic, people at that time looked to the stars and the world around them for guidance and direction. Modern-day infatuation with astrology has nothing on the love it got during the medieval era. The rich culture of using stars and other natural events to predict the future was fascinating for the people at that time. There were charts telling people what day was good to do a certain task. Dream interpretation was also a vast field that determined someone's fate. Even the movement of birds and the sound of thunder could help predict the future. If the sound came from the east, it was a warning that the upcoming year would contain bloodshed [69].

Magic in the Norse World

Religion was integrated into Norse Pagan's daily life. Magic was a regular part of that. People interacted with the gods in different ways depending on what they needed. Reciprocity was always practiced. Men and women typically performed different kinds of magic. It had more purposes in this era, and not just humans were affected. Sorcerers tried to influence the weather, animals, plants, and other elements of nature. This kind of magic required thinking of the world in a more cosmological way. They believed that every object, living or nonliving, had some kind of spirit around or within it, influencing its potential. Norse pagans associated spirits, and thus life, with all of nature, not just beings that required a heart and lungs for survival.

The ancient Germanic people worked as shamans not by defying nature but by working with it to get a certain outcome. As a result, a practitioner distinguished themselves at a higher level when their knowledge of nature's basic principles and their understanding of the client's motives and emotions was very good. Apart from these two, another type of knowledge sets a sorcerer apart from others. It was the knowledge of fate and the power of prediction. Magic is a way to achieve one's purpose, which could involve changing fate. Knowledge was a big factor in performing magic. In Old Norse, the word "Kunna" meant to know and also to have a grasp on lore and tradition. In ancient times, the word magic was called "fjölkyngi," a derivative of the word 'Kunna' [71].

Of all the subjects covered about the ancient Norsemen, information about their divination and magical practices are among the most researched by people not otherwise interested in the pagan religion. The practice of magic, during the middle ages, was not confined to the Old Norse. As just discussed it was a normal part of daily life for the average person across Europe. But the magical practices of the Norse were more integrated, accepted, and at times capable of greater things for good or bad.

The word associated with magic, most often used when discussing Norse Paganism, is divination, gaining insight into future events. Tacitus writes about it in *Germania* #10. "No people are more addicted to divination by omens and lots. The latter is performed in the following simple manner. They cut a twig from a fruit tree, and divided into small pieces, which, distinguished by certain marks, are thrown promiscuously upon a white garment... after an invocation of the gods, with his eyes lifted up to heaven, thrice takes out each piece, and, as they come up, interprets their signification according to the marks fixed upon them" [72].

The rest of #10 goes on to describe some types of divination that will, to our modern ears, sound far stranger than drawing "lots." Many ancient people watched animals for signs. At its most basic level, scientists have learned that watching animal behavior might sometimes give us hints on events to come in regard to natural disasters, but the evidence is slim. Tacitus does not give us any more information so there is no way of telling what the flight or sound of birds might have revealed to the ancient people. Tacitus talks about the actions of special milk-white horses giving clues about future events two thousand years ago, but what was magical during the Viking Era? What did it look like? How was it used? Is there magic from the Old Norse that we can access and use today?

Much of the specific occult beliefs and practices of the Vikings remain a mystery. There were divisions among the practitioners of magic, but there is very little material available on them. The faction of magic that we have more knowledge of is *seidr*. Women called *völva*, and a few "unmanly" men, practiced the high ritual magic. Much of it was related to providing help in battles [69].

Practitioners of Magic

Völur, plural for völva, were Viking women that performed magic and witchcraft. You can also call them ancient Norse seeress. Many today think of them as the Viking variant of a medieval witch. These women were not only present in the Viking age. There is evidence that they have been part of the culture for millennia [70].

The magic they performed, called seidr, means 'to bind.' The fierceness and protection, 'bound' to warriors by the völva, was carried onto the battlefield to the terror of their adversaries. Chieftains were close to their region's völva. Since they were also the spiritual head of the region, these men could practice seidr as well, but that was very uncommon. It was most likely only done when the need was immediate, and no local practitioner was available. Many of these women traveled between communities.

Völva's attire was specific. One such woman was described in the excellent book by Daniel McCoy, *The Viking Spirit*. She wore "a glass-bead necklace... a dark blue cloak... with countless precious gemstones," sewn into the fabric. Her hood was covered in "black lambskin" and "lined with white cat skin." In addition, "she held a staff with a knob on top... brass with more gemstones." Attached to her belt was "a large leather pouch," containing, "all kinds of mystifying charms." She wore "hairy calfskin shoes... and white furry cat skin gloves" [71].

If a man were to perform seidr he would be expected to wear the same, which was considered an insult to manhood. Thor, when he wore the dress to get his hammer from the giant, had to be talked into it because wearing women's clothes was looked down upon. Men who did so were called "argr," an extreme insult meaning unmanly. It is used in reference to men doing things that in their culture only women should do.

Men had physical stature and strength for power. Lacking those, a woman was free to access the power of magic in order to level the playing field.

Völva were highly respected and feared. People often turned to their personal or patron god, their "fulltrú," when seeking help or protection, but only a völva had the power to actually change their fate. It was believed that she could undo parts of fate, woven at birth by the Norns. She had the power to talk to spirits and go into different realms and dimensions. While there, she could weave the person a new fate. It was her job to discern "the course of fate and working within its structure to bring about change, which was done by symbolically weaving new events into being" [71].

One seidr ritual involved a völva being placed at the center of a group that sang very specific hymns to call in the spirits. During the singing, the völva was lifted up. She went into a trance-like state in which she shifted realms. While in that state, people asked her questions about the past and future events. The practice of seidr helped her to heal wounds, change the weather, and ensure success. Unfortunately, seidr was also used to curse people, in mild to extreme ways depending on the request of the person engaging the völva and the desires and power of the völva herself. People died as a result of curses; whether it was through actual power or the power of suggestion on the individual remains an unanswered question [70].

Their perceived ability made them extremely powerful within the community. It also made them dangerous. No one wanted to risk getting onto a völva's bad side. That is probably one of the reasons why everywhere they went, they were always given the best food to eat, the nicest bed to sleep in. No matter the request, the host did everything in his power to fulfill it and keep her happy and comfortable. Odin is known to be a master of seidr, but even he asked for advice from the völva. It was one such person who warned Odin, in Völuspá, about the final battle Ragnarök [70].

Seidr, Old Norse *seiðr,* translates to twine or cord. It was a highly ritualized event for the purpose of predicting the future and if desired, changing the fate of a group or individual. In religious prayers and ceremonies, believers seek help and intervention from a powerful deity. The practitioners of seidr, in contrast, harnessed events of fate and nature, otherwise controlled by the gods. They then used their power and knowledge to change a course of events already set into motion. "In a Norse context, magic... defined as the knowledge of how to manipulate spiritual forces and the skilled application of that knowledge in practice." There is evidence in the sagas that the prophecies of the völur came to fruition more often than not. Even if the accounts are inflated, which is a reasonable assumption, the power invoked during a seidr was both awe-inspiring and terrifying [69][71].

In addition to seidr, völva performed two other types of magic. Spá is the term used for prophesying the future based on the reading of omens or the casting of lots. The modern-day practice of reading the runes, which I will talk about shortly, is most closely aligned with this type of divination, although there is no evidence that they used small runes for casting or drawing lots at that time. The final tool völva used in performing magic was incantations which they called *galdr*. Unlike examples of how witches verbally cast spells or incantations in movies, it involved a complex mixture of vocal attributes like tone, rhythm, and volume [70].

Men also performed this type of magic. Odin is the father of galdr. Those who practiced it "combine various forms of vocalization... chanting, singing, and screaming... with care-fully chosen words," in order to bring energy to their incanta-tions. What sets this magic apart from the rest is where the source of power is perceived to come from. In a lot of magic the specific words and ingredients were the most important thing. Galdr is different. How well the magic works is depen-dent on the strength within the person preforming it. A more powerful sorcerer can bring about greater results [73] [74].

People who practiced shamanism were called shamans. Much of the work they did appears to be seidr-like or in close proximity to it. Shamans are defined as "a social functionary who... attains ecstasy in order to create a rapport with the supernatural world on behalf of his group members." In other words, they enter a trance-like state in order to interact with the spirit world on behalf of others. Based on this definition, all völva are shamans, but not all shamans are völva [75].

Shamans were influential in most non-Christian cultures. In societies around the world in which shamans were the spiritual leaders of the people, they were known to travel between the human and spirit realms. Odin is both god and shaman. As mentioned in a previous chapter, his name is a derivative from Old Norse Óðinn. This word means ecstasy and inspiration. The suffix "inn" represents mastery. So, his name directly translates to Master of Ecstasy. This ecstatic trance state is a central component of shamanism [69][75].

Shamans are said to travel with spirit and spirit animals. Odin does this with his ravens Hugin and Munin. Shamans across cultures were also known for traveling, or wandering from place to place. In the Ynglinga Saga, Odin is said to travel across far lands on missions and in his quest for ever expanding knowledge. A shaman gains their powers from a type of spiritual dying and rebirth, which Odin went through while hanging from the World Tree, Yggdrasil, in order to discover the mysteries of the runes [76].

There was a group of men who practiced magic without humiliation. They were Shamans of the battlefield, going into a trance-like state then fighting to wipe out the opposing side. They were known as berserkers, an extremely religious band of men who devoted their lives to the warrior god, Odin. Historical records give us a glimpse of what they were like. Modern doctors and scholars continue to speculate on why. They lived out in the wilderness as the animals they emulated. Depending on the group, that could be bears, wolves, or wild boars. All of which could easily tear apart any human being. They not only ate the food the animals did, but they also killed and devoured it as if they were a wild animal, tearing the prey open with their teeth and consuming it raw. The men cut off ties to their communities and lived together without shelter in packs [76].

Their frenzied violence was most likely caused by a combination of things. It is speculated that they consumed hallucinogenic mushrooms and alcohol to help enter into that state of mind. It is highly likely that at least some of them suffered from mental illness. Whatever the cause, these extreme warriors terrified all who came across them. They were at times even a danger to their own people. There are recorded cases in which a chief killed a berserker because he was too dangerous and uncontrollable [76].

Hopefully no one today aspires to be a berserker, but that doesn't mean modern society is without magic. There are no longer berserkers in the world today. That is obviously a good thing. Völva too, have all but disappeared, although I have heard of some women who are reviving the art. I've never met or talked to one personally, so I don't know how their practice as a modern-day völva compares to ones in Pre-Christian Northern Europe. There is one type of magic used by the Old Norse that is in common use today, runes.

Runes

The Futhark runes is the writing system created by the ancestors of the Vikings. It was originally made up of twenty-four symbols. Samples of it have been found in Scandinavia that date back to 160 CE. That version, called the Elder Futhark, was used until approximately 700 CE. By 790 CE an adapted sixteen symbol version, the Younger Futhark, had taken over. There is no known evidence that explains why the change was made [78].

The runic markings were meant to be inscribed in wood, on stone and even metal. Although each rune is associated with a specific sound, it was not a typical writing system. It did not have a grammatical structure. Books were not drafted in it. Stories were passed down orally, not written out for someone to read. However, there are many examples of rune sticks being carved with a message for the purpose of passing information on to someone else. The use of runes was not confined to recording words.

Like other aspects of early Norse life, the runes are woven into their mythology. Odin is a one-eyed god because he gave his other in order to gain knowledge of the runes. The physical world and the supernatural world are deeply entwined. Runes were also used in magic. Each one holds specific meaning and power. People would attach one of the symbols to something in order to imbibe the object with an added amount of whatever the rune represented. In the *Ballad of Brynhild*, Sigurth finds the Valkyrie Brynhildr in a deep sleep. She was in that state as a punishment from Odin and was grateful to be woken up. Sigurth "asked her to teach him wisdom." She does, and information about the runes are a substantial part of her instruction. "Winning runes learn, if thou longest to win. And the runes on thy sword-hilt write. Some on the furrow, and some on the flat." She goes on to tell him all the places he should put runes and which runes belong in each place [80].

Unfortunately for us, she does not give us enough information to determine the specific runes. In addition to his sword, she advises him to put the marks on his drinking horn, and both the backs and palms of his hands. They also belong on the stem, steering, and oars of boats. She mentions runes in association with many things, from newborn babies to trees, and "well-loved seats." Anywhere in which additional help, strength, or another attribute associated with a rune is desired, would be a reasonable place to put a runic symbol. It is not necessary to make them large or even visible to others. Heathens universally agree on using runes in this way but vary widely on whether or not they should be used for "fortune-telling" [80].

Within academia there is much disagreement about the true origin and use of the Futhark runes. Modern Norse pagans, who try to hold fast to the ways of the Old Norse during the Viking Age, and only that time period, find the use of the Elder Futhark runes for divination problematic. There are two reasons why, to my understanding, the first is that the Elder Futhark runes were from an earlier time than the Viking Age. The twenty-four original runes that we call the Elder Futhark stopped being used around 700 CE. This was arguably before the Viking's time. although historically not by much. The "Viking Age" was from 793 CE to 1066 CE. What followed, after 700 CE, was a shortened adapted version of the runes. The version used during that time period, called the Younger Futhark, contains only sixteen runes.

The second reason that some have a problem with using the Futhark runes is the lack of documentation of runes being used for divination purposes. The argument goes that the use of the Elder Futhark in that way is a neopagan invention. "They" meaning those people starting in the 1970s and 80s, that look to the Norse pagans and their religious beliefs for an alternative religion to the dogma of Christianity that remains dominant in the Western world. Personally, I think it's a lot of bluster with little content. Everything that we now know and do, related to the Old Norse, is a reconstruction. We have little original documentation concerning any aspect of their lives a thousand and more years ago. Does it really matter if the runes that we choose to use were from a time 1300 years ago as opposed to 1100 years ago? I do not think so, but that is just my opinion.

The argument about the ancient use of runes is, to me, a more valid argument. But again, it treats our limited knowledge and documentation as if it is complete. As I discussed in the beginning of this book, Norse paganism can and has evolved. People turn to this ancient belief system to find meaning, direction, and connection with something that will help them become better today and, in their life, moving forward. In the days of the Old Norse, slavery contributed a major part to the wealth of Vikings. No one would argue that slavery is a good thing or should be reintroduced. The thought is absurd. Likewise, when the Vikings wanted help from a god, with something very important, human sacrifice was practiced. Again, even the idea of reinstating that practice would be ludicrous. I see no need to become as dogmatic as the religion that most modern-day Norse pagans are stepping away from. For that reason, I will deal with the subject of runes as they were used historically and how they are used today. That includes the use of the twenty-four Elder Futhark runes in general, as well as runes for divination.

Runes can certainly be used in the traditional way. The Vikings engraved runes directly onto a surface or onto strips of wood and then attached that wood onto something they wanted to enhance. Heathens today place the runes in a variety of places for the same purpose. I have seen runes to promote good health in a kitchen, carved into wooden spoons used every day. They were also etched onto the bottoms of their pots and pans. For someone working their way up in the world of big business, they might put runes for strength, success, and prosperity where they hang their business attire, even engraved on a hanger itself. Runes of protection and love are put behind a child's headboard or under the bed frame.

It is important to take the time to study each rune before deciding which one to use. Some people have runes attached to almost everything around them. Most heathens put them in just a couple of places, important to them, but in a way that would not be noticeable to a non-pagan. This is especially true if family and friends are not heathens themselves.

The Old Norse did not use the runes for divination. That was clearly the realm of the völva. Most people today, who consult the runes, treat them like tarot cards. Unless you know of a völva that lives nearby that you can consult, it is a valid way to use the runes for divination today. Yes, it is a neopagan way to gain insight. If you are not comfortable with that, then my suggestion is, find something other than the runes. It is an individual choice and entirely up to you.

If you are interested in having a set of runes, there are dozens of sets available for sale. I have a set of purchased runes, but I prefer to make my own. I feel that by making them, I am imbibing them with part of myself. If you want to try your hand at making your own set of runes, visit my website listed at the back of the book. You will find a step-by-step guide on how to make them, including what materials work best. I also include a brief description of each rune and what it stands for. It is a free download, so help yourself!

Chapter 7
Celebrations, Rituals & Holidays

I began writing this book with a straightforward goal, to give heathens concrete ideas on how they can incorporate Norse paganism into their daily lives in positive, impactful ways. Holidays bring people together. They connect us with the past, our heritage, and our ancestors. How and when celebrations occur speak volumes about a group's beliefs and values. So, creating a section about the holidays we celebrate was important. Initially, I decided to only discuss the holidays that all heathens would agree should be observed within Norse paganism. If I held to that, I would have to end the discussion on holidays here.

There is little agreement on which holidays were observed, what they were called, or when they took place. Much about how the people of the North lived changed not only over time but by location. Different groups celebrated events at different times and in different ways. The holidays mentioned here are some of the most celebrated. If you celebrate different holidays or observed ones I cover in a different way, I invite you to tell me and other heathens about it on my webpage. Details on where to find it can be found at the back of this book.

Scholars agree that the Old Norse perceived the year as a wheel. It is a cycle that spins around and repeats every time the earth orbits the sun. They broke that time up into two seasons. Half the year is winter and the other half, is summer. They used a lunar calendar, divided into twelve months, each with thirty days. Instead of leap year, they handled the occasional extra day by adding four additional days, every four years in summer, a time they called, *Sumarauki*. Many of their holidays coincided with events on the lunar calendar, specifically the solstices and equinoxes. The solstices mark the longest and shortest days of the year. The equinoxes are the two days mid-point between the solstices in which the day and night are equal [81].

Societies create rituals around those things that are most important to them. Most holidays in the Western world are based on prominent events in early Christianity. That is because from the Dark Ages through much of recorded history life revolved around the church. Religion dictated almost every aspect of life in most countries across Europe.

God decided whether crops grew, or people starved. The people's responsibility was to act in a way so that God would favor them.

Survival was constantly at the forefront of thought for the Old Norse. They did not concern themselves with getting into heaven. Their needs were more immediate. If crops failed loved ones starved. An extra bad winter could mean they did not survive until spring. Their holidays and ritual reflected that reality. The ancestors of the Vikings had no concept of a structured religion in which they handed over their needs and fears to an omnipotent God. The gods were very powerful, and their help would be beneficial, but the Norse gods did not help mankind out of unconditional love. Their interaction with people was often transactional, more like a business arrangement. A specific god could provide a service, but payment was expected. "The blót was an exchange, in which they sacrificed to the gods in order to get something back in return" [82].

Blót

Payment was in the form of a sacrifice. The direct translation of sacrifice in Old Norse is *blót*. Some assume that the word has something to do with blood, but there is no connection. Snorri wrote in *Heimskringla*, about the rituals and steps of these sacrifices as it was done in Norway. In the story, Sigurd made sacrifices to the gods. The people working on farms were made to attend the event, but no outsiders were allowed. In Denmark, blóts were typically put on by the local magnates. These were the richest, most powerful men in the country, appointed by the king. They were also the major landowners. Few farmers owned the land they worked on, not just in the North but across Europe.

Blóts were typically performed in an open, high-roofed structure called a hov, or God house. Many have been found at archeological sites across Scandinavia, beneath the ruins of old Stave churches. Blóts were big affairs. It was a time for the magnates to show off their wealth. Sacrificial festivals always included a great feast. Big cauldrons were lined up over cooking fires outside the hov. After the ceremony the meat of the animal would be boiled in them, to be served to everyone present. In addition, many days were spent preparing food, especially baked goods, for the event [82].

Small animals were typically used as sacrificial offerings. For major blóts, a horse or wild hog would be killed. Human sacrifices were uncommon and given the highest honor. The blood was collected in a special container. According to Snorri, once the dish was filled with blood, the magnate used a special twig, called a *hlautteinn,* to sprinkle it across the altar and on the walls. The blood was also flung over the guests like macabre confetti. The participants did not view it that way though. The blood of a sacrifice was sacred. Being touched with it meant they were protected by the god to which the sacrifice was made. Sprinkling blood on altars and having a big feast afterward has been verified repeatedly in old text and historical research [83].

There is some doubt though on whether all the details are accurate. This is because the name of the stick used in these sacrifices, hlautteinn, was also the name for the one used in predicting the future, during divination rituals. There is often a problem in figuring out exactly how things were done without the benefit of real-time documentation, and people can get it wrong. For example, misdiagnosing the purpose of "the twig," the hlautteinn reminds me of a scene in the Disney movie, *The Little Mermaid* when Ariel wrongly uses a fork because she was told that it was something used to comb her hair [84]. It is important to use evidence to figure out what items were for, or how things were done. But it is just as important, if not more, to acknowledge when new insight leads us in a different direction.

After blessing the alter, people, and building, with the blood from the sacrifice, the blót continued with a toast. Most often the toast was to Odin, but Njörðr and Freyr were also gods to commemorate. They were associated with the fertility of the land and having a good harvest. After a toast to the gods, they would engage in Bragafull and Minni. Both of which are rituals that involve toasting and drinking [83].

Bragafull, or *bragarfull*, was the time for making oaths. It was a bold, public, announcement of their intent to do something big and impressive. The event started by drinking alcohol from longhorns, also called bragafull, after toasting a god. The leader would take the first drink and then make his proclamation to all those in attendance. Then the bragafull horn was passed around, everyone taking a drink in turn. Oaths were not to be taken lightly. Once someone has made an oath to do something, they must succeed, or their honor and reputation will be destroyed. Many oaths ended with the fateful words, "or die trying." It was one such oath that led to the death of a very famous Viking.

The Saga of Ragnar Lothbrok is the story of a Viking king. At a bragafull, he stood and made an oath that he would retake England with only two ships. Whether it was made as a result of too much mead or underestimating his foe, it was a fateful vow. Ragnar sailed to England with just two longboats full of warriors. He is quickly captured by King Ælla of Northumbria. The details of Ragnar's death are well-known to most Old Norse enthusiasts. Thrown into a pit full of poisonous snakes, his demise was slow and painful. The skaldic poem Krákumál, or The Death-Song of Ragnar Lothbrok, supposedly gives us his final words. He is jovial even as he slowly dies from the venom, regaling those present with a litany of his heroic achievements. He also voices the hope that his sons will avenge him, which they later do. The poem ends with, "laughing I shall die," and so he does [85].

Another part of a blót, before the feast, is Minni. Minni is the act of remembering. It was the time, during sacrificial festivals, to remember the dead. Ancestor veneration is a prominent feature of Norse pagan beliefs. We survive thanks to the hard work and knowledge of those that came before us. That is as true today as it was in the Viking Era. For the Old Norse though the ancestors continue to help them long after death. To keep them happy and willing to assist the living it was important to praise and thank the ancestors [86].

There was originally more to the blót ceremony based on stanza 144 of the Havamal. Several extra traditions related to sacrificial rituals are mentioned there, but we do not have enough information to know how it was all done. The person performing the blót was expected to be knowledgeable about more than just how to sacrifice an animal. The stanza says, "whether a person knows how to carve, how to paint, how to ask and advise, how to bid and send, and how to slaughter" [87].

Sumbel

Blóts were intense affairs. They were a physical manifestation of the Norse concept of reciprocity. The people wanted something from a god or gods. Blood was spilled. Life was taken as an offering, "payment" in advance for what they hoped they would receive in exchange from the gods.

Sumbels, on the other hand, were loud, boisterous affairs with lots of drinking and storytelling. There are no sacrifices. Sumbels are the time for giving thanks for the fulfillment, by the gods, of the requests for assistance made during blót. They are exhilarating to participate in. In addition to friendship and camaraderie, it's a time to praise the gods, talk about shared interests and beliefs and revel in the sense of belonging. "A Sumbel is a formal drinking ritual composed of toasting, hails, oath-taking, the recitation of poetry or song, and other forms of verbal expression" [88].

People traveled great distances to attend Sumbel celebrations. It was a good time to make alliances, arrange marriages and hash out business agreements. Bragafull and minni were part of the celebration. In addition to remembering the ancestors during minni, the tradition is also linked to remembering past events. With a drinking horn in hand, the one speaking entertained the audience with detailed descriptions of how their oath was fulfilled. Once they achieved their goal it was time to boast about their accomplishments. "Boasting in this case is not the empty claims and exaggerations we normally associate with the word, but an acknowledging of our own accomplishments and the help of the Gods and ancestors." For Norse pagans, there is nothing wrong with boasting about yourself, so long as you tell the truth when expounding on what you have achieved. It was also important to thank the specific god that helped you along the way [89].

Holidays

Now that the groundwork has been laid, it is time to jump into specific holidays. Whether you want to celebrate "Christian" holidays and focus on the pagan elements of the festivities, or you would rather confine yourself to purely Norse Pagan events, there are plenty of celebrations to go around. Like everything else connected to the Old Norse, it is impossible to know exactly how each holiday was celebrated. The reality is, even if we knew every detail, we would not celebrate them exactly as the Old Norse did. After all, animal and sometimes human sacrifice was often part of celebrations.

Most of us grew up celebrating a set group of holidays, mostly Christian holidays. Schools closed; airports were packed with families returning home to grandma's house to share all the annual traditions. As a heathen, Norse Pagan, or pagan in general, you may feel a little trepidation about continuing to celebrate holidays that belong to another religious tradition. Many holidays that we celebrate today have pagan origins. Some go all the way back to ancient Rome. During the spread of Christianity, many pagan holidays were incorporated into existing religious holidays, approved by the church.

Scholars have tried to separate out the specific parts of pagan holidays, from the ancient world, that have been incorporated into the holidays we celebrate today. Many of them were modified from the beginning, others were brought in whole but later whittled down to a recognizable version. Sometimes similar traditions came from multiple sources. To provide a clear sequence of events, from an original pagan form through its many transformations to the recognizable, mainstream holiday custom we celebrate today is difficult. Different practices, from many cultures, were blended into the holidays. Ancient Norse and Celtic traditions are deeply entwined with many traditions that we think of as purely Christian [90].

Scholars have tried to untangle the origin of specific items and events that people have come to see as intrinsic parts of major holidays. Which parts, of pagan holiday activities from the ancient world, have been transformed and incorporated into the holidays we celebrate today? Even for them, it is difficult to always draw clear lines of influence. Often several regions will claim to be the starting point for the same tradition. I will use one bit, or bite, of a traditional Christmas decoration to demonstrate the issue. Where do you think the tradition of decorating fancy gingerbread houses and little icing-dressed cookie-men at Christmas comes to us from? The most popular explanation is that it began after the German Grimm brothers published their famous tale of Hansel and Gretel. So, it obviously comes to us from Germany, right? Not so fast. Three other countries also have valid claims to the tradition, Britain, France, and the Netherlands. There is no one right answer [91].

The reason I bring this up is that many of the traditions that can be legitimately traced back to the ancient Norse can also be traced back to other groups as well. For the purpose of this chapter, I am not going to go into those alternate versions. In claiming a Norse origin for certain traditions, I do not mean it in any way to take away from the legitimate claim of others to the same or similar traditions. Even something as simple as chicken soup has a multi-cultural background.

Similarities between Modern and Pagan Holidays

Growing up in the United States, most of us celebrated the typical "Christian" holidays. Things in your life may change when you become a Norse pagan but celebrating the holidays does not have to be one of them. Like using the runes for divination, it is a personal choice. Not only can you celebrate the ones you choose, but you will enjoy and be more connected with them knowing most of these holidays have pagan origins.

Yule and Christmas

Christmas time contains a mix of several pagans' holiday traditions, not just the Norse. Winter was a brutal time. People spent their days with little to do, huddled together inside their homes waiting for the harsh weather to improve enough that they could once again venture outside for any length of time. They had to survive on food and firewood that had been saved during the rest of the year. During the darkest days of winter, the Norse people celebrated the coming light. Each day, since the summer solstice, was a bit shorter and darker. By the winter solstice, especially in the North, it was dark far more than it was light. The solstice marks the point where that begins to change. Moving forward, each day lasts a little longer, until the next summer solstice. At the winter solstice, it is at the lowest point, from which it will again rise. The wheel continues to turn year after year [90].

The Vikings called the holiday *Yule*. The winter solstice is a time of festivities. *Yule* let them enjoy life and forget their problems for a while. It was a great celebration that lasted for days. Heavy drinking was a must. So much so, that the first Christian king of Norway, King Haakon, actually mandated that the people partied and consumed massive amounts of alcohol. It was a time of comradery with friends and family. The king promoted the tradition of having a special feast. That custom is the origin of the special Christmas dinner that families share each year. In addition to mandating a good time, Haakon did not push his subjects to change religions. No wonder they called him "Haakon the Good" [92].

Many Christmas traditions come from this holiday. The tradition of gift-giving to family and friends at Yule was as important then as it is today at Christmas. Multiple countries had a version of Santa Claus. For the Old Norse, it was Odin. He rode across the sky in his chariot pulled by his eight-legged horse, Sleipnir. He left small gifts in the shoes of good boys and girls. Even the idea of Santa coming down the chimney originated with the Old Norse. Their homes were built with a hole in the roof for smoke to escape through. When snow became so deep that they could not get in or out through the door, they had no choice but to climb through the hole in the roof [93].

Their homes were decorated with evergreen boughs and lots of candles. There is symbolism in both. Evergreen trees never lose leaves or appear to die, even in winter. It was a sign of nature's annual rebirth. The candles represented the light that would, from then until the summer solstice, increase with each day. They sang and recited poetry in booming voices, like the way Christmas carols can sound after a few too many spiked eggnogs. As the day turned into night, bonfires were lit up around the area, short distances apart, representing the sun [90].

The oldest tradition of Yule was making the Yule log, that ritual spread all over northern Europe. An evergreen tree was carefully chosen and cut down. It was then dragged back to the longhouse in a great procession. One end of the tree was put into the hearth and burnt. The tree would burn down, and a member of the family would push more of the tree in until it had burnt for 12 days. At that time, the fire was put out and the leftover semi-burnt log would be used to light the fire the following year. In Holland, it was common to place the remaining log under the bed until the next Yule. They believed that doing so would prevent lightning from striking the home [94].

I cannot imagine a traditional Christmas celebration without a Christmas tree. This practice was not only inspired by Norse paganism but also by Roman and Druidic traditions. Winter in the North was the most dangerous season for the Old Norse. Evergreen trees are strong, green, and continue to stand even in the harshness of snowfall and frigid weather. It was a perfect symbol of the strength and endurance that people needed at the time. It was also a sign of fertility. At Yule, they brought a small fir tree into their homes and decorated it with candles, golden apples, and balls [94].

For the Old Norse, the holiday tree was also a reminder of the World Tree, Yggdrasil. It contains the entire Norse universe within its branches. All nine realms or worlds, the sun, moon, ocean, everything is there. Various mythical and real creatures live in and around the tree, each with a task that they continually perform. From a Christian perspective, they viewed the happenings within the mythical tree as a constant struggle between good and evil. The Old Norse did not think in terms of good and evil, but they believed strongly in the concept of reciprocity. If one took, another gave, then the taker in turn, became the giver to another. In this way, nature and the world stayed in balance. Within the tree, is an entire ecosystem that is constantly in a cycle of reciprocity. The decorations placed on the tree represented the sun, moon, and other parts of the universe found in Yggdrasil [95][94].

New Year's Resolutions

Vikings sat around the fire, told stories, and made oaths. Making oaths was always a big part of the Yule celebration. An oath is basically a public proclamation in which a person states that they are going to do a certain thing. It was often done in the name of or dedicated to a god. The Old Norse felt strongly about the importance of keeping your word. As previously mentioned, it is a common topic in Norse mythology. The oaths, that were made during the Yule celebration, began the tradition of making New Year's resolutions [90].

Easter Bunny

When you think of Easter, you probably think of the resurrection of Jesus and somehow a rabbit spreading around chocolate eggs. What is the connection between Jesus and the bunny? The rabbit is not from Christian history but an amalgamation of several beings of pagan origin. Stories from the Middle Ages describe a Germanic goddess named Eostre. She was a fertility goddess over birth and the soil. She had pet rabbits and other rabbits served her. Rabbits are well known for producing a huge number of offspring every year, so there is a strong connection with fertility.

A story about the goddess explains one part of today's Easter festivities. One year, Eostre delayed the onset of spring, which caused a bird to die, freezing in the snow. Taking pity on the bird, she turned it into a rabbit who then hopped across the land. It was known for leaving multicolored eggs in special nests, made by children.

When German immigrants arrived in Pennsylvania, they brought the story with them. With time, the tradition came to include chocolate and other small gifts. Baskets later replaced homemade nests for convenience. Next time, when the holiday comes around, remember the story of the original Easter Bunny. Eat some eggs, enjoy your chocolate and give thanks to the goddess Eostre for blessing the earth, and making it fertile [95].

Ashes at Lent

Lent is a Christian religious holiday of repentance. Christians get ashes pressed to their forehead on this day. This tradition was inspired by Norse mythology. In one myth, a hero named

Sigurd kills a monster. He gains unbelievable strength when he washes in its blood. Unfortunately, he forgets one spot on his arm. This part is later pierced by an arrow containing poison, and he dies because of it. Later in the myth, his corpse is burnt on a pyre. The cremation process turned his body into ash. Norse associated ashes with the ashes of this hero and used them to represent power. Norse shamans used to place ash on a person's head as a blessing and call for protection from the gods. Placing ash on someone can symbolize repentance or strength based on the religious tradition being followed [96].

"Pagan Only" Holidays

I have talked about some Christian holidays with pagan roots, but what about holidays outside of the Christian realm? Solstices and equinoxes were commemorated every year with celebrations, festivals, and feasts. Beyond that, there is no definitive list of Old Norse holidays, but there are some that are regularly celebrated by heathens today. Usually, the original practice died out but was revived as paganism began attracting followers again in the 1900s. The events were reconstructed by different individuals or groups, each with their own interpretation of how and when they should be celebrated. It would be almost impossible to present all the different variations. The following holidays are ones that are enjoyed by many within the heathen community. I list them in consecutive order, but my starting point was random. When a new year began, according to the Vikings, is unknown. They did not have a "New Year" celebration.

One part of our understanding of Forn siðr, the customs of the Old Norse, that is incomplete, concerns which events typically involved sumbels and which required blóts. There are only two "official" blóts that we have significant information about. Those are Álfablót, the elves blót and Dísablót, a blót dedicated to the dísir. There are many references to sacrifices being performed in the Eddas, but they are rarely connected to specific days of the year. Whether or not a given celebration incorporates a sumbel or blót, every celebration involved making toasts to the gods. Here are some lines from a medieval poem that may have been used on such occasions.

> *Hail to the gods!*
> *Hail to the goddesses!*
> *Hail to the bounteous earth!*
> *Speech and wit*
> *Give to us famous ones*
> *And healing hands, while we live!* [97]

Charming of the Plow/ Disting

The holiday takes place in early February, at the first full moon. It was the time when people began to clean and repair their tools, clear the land of scrub and overgrowth, and get ready for the planting season. Although still cold outside, it was when people started to look forward to spring. This holiday also commemorates the cunning wisdom of Gefjun, goddess of the plow. According to legend, she is responsible for creating the Danish Island of Zealand. Gefjun plays a part in several mythical stories but the one relevant to the holiday Disting or Charming of the Plow is *The Deluding of Gylfi,* in the Prose Edda [98].

King Gylfi came across a beggarwoman who entertained him with her wit and personality. As a reward, he gifted her a "ploughland." That meant that she would own whatever land she was able to plow by herself in one day, with the help of four Oxen. The king probably thought he was giving her a small farmstead at the most. What the king did not know was that the beggar was actually a powerful goddess. She magically transformed her four sons into massive oxen. They plowed so deep and wide that they dug a lake and created a large island. The "lake" refers to the sea between the island and the mainland on either side. Considering its mythical origin, the island is truly massive in size. It is an ancient story, but one that should still impress modern heathens. Take a few minutes on Google Earth and look at the city of Copenhagen, Denmark, then pan out. You will discover that the entire city, including suburbs, only takes up a small part of the island of Zealand [87].

Dísablót is performed during Charming of the Plow celebrations, in honor of the dísir, who are powerful female spirits. Within Norse mythology, dísir are both warriors and protectors. Some say they are female landvættir, land wights in English. Many heathens believe that a landvættir is the form our ancestors, that stick around to watch over us, take. Others say that a dísir is a Valkyrie. Freyja has been referred to as a dísir. The lines are blurred. The only thing we know for sure is that they are always female. According to Daniel McCoy, author of Viking Spirit, "The Disir are often depicted as the spirits of dead female ancestors, which suggests a considerable degree of overlap with the elves, who are often characterized likewise" [99]. That kind of ambiguity is not uncommon. Often a single entity is described as being several different things.

The Old Norse performed sacrifices at this time in hope that the dísir would bless the land with fertility so that they could grow enough food in the coming year to survive the next winter. The traditional way to celebrate the holiday was for people to have the tools of their trade, often a plow, blessed in the name of the dísir. People sang songs. Many of which have survived to modern times in Scandinavia [98].

Ostara

Easter incorporated many aspects of Ostara into its festivities. As a result, this holiday shares many traditions with modern

Easter celebrations. I talked about some of them earlier when discussing that holiday. Ostara is celebrated around the spring equinox. The goddess of spring and fertility, Eostre, is strongly tied to this holiday. The animal she is most closely associated with is the hare, so rabbits may have played a role in the celebration. There are lots of activities involving eggs, which represent fertility. They were decorated, hidden and found, and eaten just like Easter eggs. There were races with children carrying eggs. They were even put in baskets or homemade nests. There was singing and dancing. Poems were recited and stories about fertility gods and goddesses were told. It was an exciting time. All of those present had survived the dark months and were eager to embrace the light of a new season. This is the holiday to praise Mother Earth and the goddess Eostre for birthing new life after the harshness of winter.

For the Old Norse, the god Baldr is closely tied to this holiday. Many believe he is reborn during Ostara, after being killed in winter, during the time the holiday Vetrnætr is observed. Sometimes heathens will commemorate this, and other stories connected to the holiday, through lively reenactments. Not all reenactments may be family-friendly though. At some celebrations, "a woman and a man are chosen to act out the roles of Spring God and Goddess, playing out courtship and symbolically planting seeds" [101].

Midsummer's Day/ Sumarmál

The summer solstice is when the holiday Sumarmál, also called Midsummer's Day, is celebrated. Despite the name, it takes place around the third week of June, not the middle of summer. Midsummer's Day was considered the second most important celebration of the year to the Vikings. Yule being the first. Huge bonfires were lit.

Sumarmál celebrates the turning of one season to the next. It marks the last day of winter and the first day of summer. At this point in the year, crops have been planted and warriors are preparing to plunder distant lands. According to Ynglinga Sága, sacrifices were to be made at this time. It was important to ask the gods to bless them so that they were successful in their raids and returned safely home afterward. Blóts were a form of payment to the gods for their protection and good fortune [102].

The Vikings also participated in ritual bathing at this time to wash away any misfortune that may have settled on them. With raiding season about to begin, it is understandable that they would want to be rid of any bad luck that could wreak havoc in the months to come. Animal bones were tossed into the roaring fires It the hope that the smoke would keep away unsavory spirits that might want to do them harm. It has been speculated that a "bonfire" was originally called a "bone-fire," named after this practice [103].

In Scandinavian countries, Sumarmál, although with a different name in each country, continues to be extremely popular. Partying around bonfires is a common way to celebrate across the region, but each country has its own unique traditions that coincide with the holiday. In Denmark people who work in the healing arts spend the day collecting medicinal herbs that were needed for the year. In Finland, a woman, who is not yet married, will collect "seven different flowers and place them under her pillow to dream of her future husband." A tradition unique to Norway is to hold mock weddings, "meant to symbolize the blossoming of new life." In Sweden, the holiday is celebrated in a variety of ways including, "Raising and dancing around a maypole," dressed in traditional clothing, while singing well-known folk songs. Specific foods are eaten, and heavy drinking is expected. They also follow the same custom as Finland, of putting seven flowers under the pillow of women who want a glimpse of their future husband [103].

Vetrnætr

Vetrnætr, also called Winternights, is a celebration to mark the end of the summer and the beginning of the winter half of the year. Many celebrate Samhain around this same time. This is one of the specific holidays mentioned in Ynglinga Sága, and it requires a blót. It is when the Haustblót, or autumn sacrifice, was performed [104].

Based on its mention in the lore, we can assume it was a widely observed event, but not a lot is known about how this holiday was traditionally celebrated. Since it required a blót there would be bragafull and minni; oaths and toasts made, ancestors and deeds remembered. It was the time to slaughter animals needed for food during the winter, so that may have been incorporated into the Haustblót sacrifice. "It is also a time to give a portion of what we have gained over the summer as both thanks and as a petition for a favorable winter." The lore tells us that "Freyr, Óðinn, the álfar, and the dísir," are to be honored at this time [104].

The veil between the physical and the spirit world was thought to be thinnest at this time of year. So, it was a good time to talk about, and to, those who have passed on. It was a time to light bonfires, share in a feast, give thanks and celebrate the fall harvest. An old prayer, to be recited during Winternights, has survived. "Til árs ok friðar." Which translates to, "for a good year and peace" [105].

Krampusnacht

Krampusnacht is not Halloween, but if you were out during the celebration, you might notice a similarity. In Germany, there is a "bad Santa" type character named Krampus. December fifth is his night. He is an ugly, horned creature with a very long tongue. Unlike Santa, in search of good little boys and girls to give gifts to, Krampus is on the hunt for the naughty ones. He carries a birch switch and a large sack. When he comes across a child who is badly behaved, he beats them. Then he scoops them into his sack and takes them away, so their family no longer must deal with such misbehavior.

Every year partiers dress up as Krampus and parade around town. Some carry sticks and pretend to be on the lookout for troublesome kids. Parents give them schnaps to bribe "Krampus" and keep their children safe. The whole family may be out and about this night, but unlike Halloween, on Krampusnacht it is adults who dress up and are given treats [88].

Yule

We have already discussed it in relation to Christmas. Yule begins on the winter solstice and lasts for twelve days. Baking loaves of bread and sweets, as well as brewing ale or mead, were common activities this time of year. The food and drink were shared later, during the festivities. Singing songs and reciting poetry was enjoyed by all. Still trapped in the dark embrace of winter, Yule was the time to bring in the light. Bonfires were lit outside, and Yule logs burned in the hearth. Evergreen sprigs and fir trees were decorated reminding all that life continued, even as winter stormed outside [90].

Even if we knew every detail of how holidays were commemorated a thousand years ago, we would not celebrate them exactly as the Old Norse did. As Norse Paganism continues to evolve, it is acceptable to use modern substitutions for the Old Ways, so long as the spirit of the event remains true.

Holidays are meant to be enjoyed with others. If you do not have friends or family that share your enthusiasm for Norse Paganism, I encourage you to step out of your comfort zone. Create an informal group or join one. If you are unsure of which holidays to celebrate, I suggest beginning with the solstices and equinoxes. If you live in an area with a sizable population, there are bound to be some pagan activities going on.

Chapter 8
Being Norse Pagan Today

The traits and values in Norse Paganism can help you build a happy, successful, fully engaged life. Throughout this book, I have discussed how the Old Norse viewed the world around them. More importantly, how the customs and values of the Old Norse can benefit people in their lives today.

There is a disconnect among many in the Western world between what they profess as their values and how they live their lives, outside of their place of worship or the presence of other worshippers. It is understandable. Being meek, subservient, and blindly obedient is not a satisfying life for most people.

I am not a Christian scholar, but I went to several websites, run by Christian organizations, that use verses from the bible to answer questions about Christianity. I typed in the question, "What is the best way to live your life?" My criteria for which scriptures to include here was straightforward. The same biblical verse had to be among the answers to my question on at least three of the websites. Here is what I learned [106].

Christians are supposed to live as Jesus lived. "Whoever claims to live in him must live as Jesus did" (1 John 2:6). "For I have given you an example, that you also should do just as I have done to you" (John 13:15).

They are expected to be meek, humble, and gentle. "In humility count others more significant than yourselves" (Philippians 2:3). "What does the Lord require of you but to do justice, and to love kindness, and to walk humbly with your God?" (Micah 6:8). "Put on compassion, kindness, humility, gentleness, and patience" (Colossians 3:12). "Make it your ambition to lead a quiet life: You should mind your own business and work with your hands, just as we told you" (1 Thessalonians 4:11). "Let your gentleness be evident to all" (Philippians 4:5).

Expect to be treated badly. Do not stand up for your self or fight back. "Therefore I take pleasure in infirmities, in reproaches, in needs, in persecutions, in distresses, for Christ's sake. For when I am weak, then I am strong" (2 Corinthians 12:10). "If someone slaps you on the right cheek, offer the other cheek also. If you are sued in court and your shirt is taken from you, give your coat, too." (Matthew 5:39-40).

Christians should become child-like. "Unless you change and become like little children, you will never enter the kingdom of heaven. Therefore, whoever takes the lowly position of this child is the greatest in the kingdom of heaven" (Matthew 18:3-4). "Therefore be imitators of God, as beloved children" (Ephesians 5:1).

The next life is most important. Christians should not befriend or love the earth. "You unfaithful people! Don't you know that friendship with the world means hostility toward God? So whoever wants to be the world's friend becomes God's enemy" (James 4:4). "Do not love the world or the things in the world. If anyone loves the world, the love of the Father is not in them" (1 John 2:15). "Therefore I take pleasure in infirmities, in reproaches, in needs, in persecutions, in distresses, for Christ's sake. For when I am weak, then I am strong" (2 Corinthians 12:10). "Do not love the world or anything in the world" (Luke 12:15). "Set your minds on things that are above, not on things that are on earth" (Colossians 3:2).

Christians should not desire money or expensive possessions. "Sell your possessions and give to those in need... Where your treasure is, there your heart will be too" (Luke 12:33-34). "Jesus said to him, 'If you want to be perfect, go, sell what you have and give to the poor, and you will have treasure in heaven;

and come, follow Me" (Matthew 19:21). "Your way of life should be free from the love of money, and you should be content with what you have" (Hebrews 13:5). "But I say, walk by the Spirit, and you will not gratify the desires of the flesh" (Galatians 5:16).

Good Christians are not to trust their own judgment or ask questions. "Do all things without grumbling or questioning, that you may be blameless and innocent, children of God" (Philippians 2:14-15). "Trust in the Lord with all your heart and lean not on your own understanding" (Proverbs 3:5).

It is wrong for women to dress up and look nice. She should not draw attention to herself by looking stylish or well put together. "I also want the women to dress modestly, with decency and propriety, adorning themselves, not with elaborate hairstyles or gold or pearls or expensive clothes" (Timothy 2:9-10). "Your beauty should not come from outward adornment, such as braided hair and the wearing of gold jewelry and fine clothes" (1 Peter 3:2-5).

The bible teaches that Christians should be satisfied with what they have, instead of wanting more. "Let your character be free from the love of money, being content with what you have" (Hebrews 13:15). "Be content with your wages" (Luke 3:14). "But if we have food and clothing, with these we will be content" (1 Timothy 6: 8) [106].

According to Google, there are over two billion Christians in the world today. Common sense leads me to believe that there are millions, hundreds of millions of devout Christians, who consider the bible one hundred percent factual, who find that "child-like" life appealing, with a "Father" firmly in control. They feel secure in having clear set boundaries and rules to follow. For those that do, living a Christian life is probably very rewarding.

I am not disparaging Christianity. I am merely showing the differences in core beliefs between the two, Norse paganism and Christianity so that people can decide for themselves what works best for their own lives.

Obedience without questioning, being satisfied with a life of labor without striving for the nice things that hard work can provide, is not for everyone. It certainly is not for me. I respect every person's right to choose the religion that they feel is right and true for them. Likewise, that same acceptance should be given to people in every religion. It is possible for us to have mutual respect without believing in the same deities or ideologies.

For most Norse pagans a life of deference, without the pursuit of upward career mobility is not satisfying in a sustainable way. Neither is continuous self-sacrifice without the benefit of rewards. It is good to help others and do charitable work, but it should be in balance with the rest of your life. For example, you may spend weekends helping to build homes for the charity Habitat for Humanity. For many, it would be satisfying and worthwhile. But at the end of the day, when you head back home to the house of your dreams, enjoy the comforts of living there without guilt. You worked hard for it and deserve to enjoy the fruits of your labor.

Despite what the bible says, most Christians do not live self-less lives. Those that do are acting in obedience to what their God has told them to do. They have set aside their own wishes, dreams, and desires in order to please their God. If you are a Christian, that is admirable.

The gods in the Norse pantheon, have more realistic expectations of their followers. What they value is different. If a heathen's desire is to please the gods, they will act in a way consistent with their gods' values. I have discussed those values and priorities throughout the book. In talking about the relationship between the Old Norse and modern military values, the importance of courage, facing your fears, honor, honesty, reliability, and faithfulness were expounded on.

In learning about their holidays, we can see the emphasis the Old Norse placed on acknowledging the reality of a current situation with a hopeful eye toward the future. The festival of Yule took place during the dark, frozen winter, but they toasted the gods and lit bonfires to celebrate the sun and warmth to come. Reciprocity is central to how Norse pagans deal with each other and the world at large. They are very much in and of the world. The earth gives us so much. As modern heathens, we have an obligation to repay that debt by taking care of the planet and the environment.

Germania was written two thousand years ago, but already the traits most important to the Germanic people and later to their progeny, the Vikings, were on display. You learned that leaders led by example, not decree. Norse Pagans are leaders. A good leader displays many traits that are highly praised in Norse paganism, whether they are pagan or not. They give 100% of themselves. They are at the front of the battlelines, not hiding behind subordinates in case things do not go the way they plan. They value their employees and let the employees know that they are valued. Tacitus, in *Germania*, discusses this concept. "Their generals command less through the force of authority, then of example. If they are daring, adventurous, and conspicuous in action, they procure obedience from the admiration they inspire." Of course, Norse pagans are followers too, but they do not follow blindly [107].

Husbands valued and respected their wives and listened to their council. They did not have affairs. "Clandestine correspondence is equally unknown to men and women." They took responsibility for the well-being of their families. The people of Germania had no use for slackers or liars. "No one in Germany laughs at vice, nor do they call it the fashion to corrupt and to be corrupted" [107].

Living an entirely selfless life is not the life that a Norse pagan typically desires. Norse Pagans take charge of their life. They are at the front pushing forward. How they do that depends on the issues most dear to their hearts. For some that might mean living out in the country, getting back to nature, growing their own food, and raising their family to be self-sufficient. For another, it might mean working hard to build a career that utilizes the traits of the gods such as determination, honesty, and fearless offense instead of reactionary defense.

The hávamál is full of good advice on how we should live our lives. "A better burden may no man bear for wanderings wide than wisdom; It is better than wealth on unknown ways, and in grief a refuge it gives." Never stop learning. Odin wandered the realms in search of greater wisdom. A child on the first day of school or a retired bus driver who has always wanted to go to college can each look to Odin. Through him, they know that learning and wisdom are needed to achieve what you want in life. It is important to put in the work and build a strong foundation on which to build the life you want. Learning and through it, wisdom can also be a goal in itself. "Wise shall he seem who well can question, and also answer well" [108].

There are so many things to learn about. Do not limit yourself to just the information needed to do your job. "A measure of wisdom each man shall have, but never too much let him know; The fairest lives do those men live whose wisdom wide has grown."

It is important to stand up and help when you see a wrong being done, especially towards those who cannot stand up for themselves. The idea is contained in one of the most revered and recited quotes from the hávamál "Where you recognize evil, speak out against it, and give no truces to your enemies." The saying hangs on the walls of innumerable heathen homes [108].

The smart, strong, silent type describes many Norse, both old and new. "The son of a king shall be silent and wise, and bold in battle as well; Bravely and gladly a man shall go, till the day of his death is come." People of all ages are drawn to that type of person. It is why the Norse gods are popular today in books and movies, regardless of the audience's beliefs [108].

An ignorant person doesn't bother learning because they think they already know everything. The Definition of "ignorant" isn't someone with a low IQ or a lack of formal education. According to Wikipedia, "The word 'ignorant' is an adjective that describes a person in the state of being unaware or even cognitive dissonance... and can describe individuals who are unaware of important information or facts" [109].

An ignorant person will talk about something as if it is a fact without taking the time to investigate it and gather the truth from reliable sources. Our country right now is divided. Both sides are guilty of being willfully "ignorant" of all the facts, especially if the facts do not line up with what they already believe. Odin cautions against that type of thinking. "An ignorant man thinks that all he knows when he sits by himself in a corner; But never what answer to make he knows when others with questions come" [108].

The hávamál cautions us against mocking others. "A paltry man and poor of mind at all things ever mocks. For never he knows, what he ought to know, that he is not free from faults." A Norse pagan does not feel the need to add something to every conversation or always have the last word. "Often he speaks who never is still with words that win no faith; The babbling tongue, if a bridle it find not, oft for itself sings ill." Nobody is an expert at everything. "A witless man, when he meets with men, had best in silence abide; For no one shall find that nothing he knows, if his mouth is not open too much. But a man knows not, if nothing he knows, when his mouth has been open too much." A person, who is not very smart, tends to give themselves away without even being aware of it. Odin cautions us against that behavior [108].

It is fine to boast about achievements but avoid bragging about how smart you are. Let your deeds speak for you. "A man shall not boast of his keenness of mind, but keep it close in his breast; To the silent and wise does ill come seldom" [108].

The hávamál teaches us how to be good guests. "The cautious guest who comes to the table speaks sparingly, listens with ears, learns with eyes. Such is the seeker of knowledge," and "Go you must. No guest shall stay in one place forever. Love will be lost If you sit too long at a friend's fire" [108].

It gives us guidance on how to be a good host. "Fire he needs who with frozen knees has come from the cold without; Food and clothes must the farer have, the man from the mountains come." If someone is under our roof, it is our responsibility to make sure that their needs are met. "Water and towels and welcoming speech should he find who comes, to the feast" [108].

Be an upstanding, honest, reliable person. For Norse Pagans having a good reputation is extremely important. "Cattle die, and kinsmen die, and so one dies one's self; but a noble name will never die, if good renown one gets... One thing now that never dies, the fame of a dead man's deeds [108].

It is important to pay your debt and pay back what someone has loaned you. "None so free with gifts or food have I found that gladly he took not a gift, nor one who so widely scattered his wealth that of recompense hatred he had" [108].

The hávamál gives us advice on how to live a good life. Stay healthy. Overeating is not a good thing to do. "The greedy man, if his mind be vague, will eat till sick he is; The vulgar man, when among the wise, to scorn by his belly is brought," or said another way, "The herds know well when home they shall fare, and then from the grass they go; But the foolish man his belly's measure shall never know aright" [108].

Friendship, companionship, and community are important. We are not meant to spend life all alone. "Sorrow eats the heart if you cannot tell someone your whole mind." We need to be able to share what is in our hearts with others. "Affection is mutual when men can open all their heart to each other." The person can be a friend, a sibling, a spouse, or even a mentor. "Young was I once, and wandered alone, and naught of the road I knew; Rich did I feel when a comrade I found, for man is man's delight." It is a basic human need to seek love and acceptance. "On the hillside drear the fir-tree dies, all bootless its needles and bark; It is like a man whom no one loves. Why should his life be long?" [108].

The Old Norse understood that it was important to be a good friend for friendships to last. Make time for the people you care about. "Profit thou hast if thou hearest, great thy gain if thou learnest: if a friend thou hast whom thou fully wilt trust, then fare to find him oft; For brambles grow and waving grass on the rarely trodden road." True friends are precious; Value them. "Be never the first to break with thy friend the bond that holds you both." Friends do not require extravagant gifts to know that they are important to you. It is the little things that show you care. "No great thing needs a man to give, oft little will purchase praise. With half a loaf and a half-filled cup, a friend full fast I made." That is true especially when you have shared interests or values [108].

Go to bed at a reasonable time. "For rudeness none shall rightly blame you if soon your bed you seek." Don't let the worries of the day stop you from sleeping. "The witless man is awake all night, thinking of many things. Care-worn he is when the morning comes, and his woe is just as it was" [108].

The physical strength that was needed a thousand years ago is no longer necessary for survival. At the same time, working out, and building a strong powerful body can be done in praise of Thor. It is also a way to manifest, in a physical way, the traits of the Old Norse that you embrace. This is not a religion for the weak or lazy, or those unable to make decisions for themselves. That has nothing to do with physical strength. A woman in a wheelchair can be a powerful CEO in any boardroom. A heathen midwife, helping women give birth at home surrounded by their loved ones, does so with prayers to Freyja on her lips. Someone in the military or law enforcement can look to the god Heimdall, "guardian of the Bifrost Bridge and watchman of the Aesir," for strength and courage while on the job [110].

A good leader displays many traits that are highly praised in Norse Paganism, whether they are pagan or not. They give 100% of themselves. They are at the front of the battlelines, not hiding behind subordinates in case things don't go the way they plan. They value their employees and let the employees know that they are valued. Tacitus, in *Germania* 7, discusses this concept. "Their generals command less through the force of authority, then of example. If they are daring, adventurous, and conspicuous in action, they procure obedience from the admiration they inspire" [108].

Many, if not most modern Norse Pagans practice their religion in solitude. I suspect that will continue to be the case, but I want to encourage you to reach out to other Norse Pagans and heathens. Make new friends and create new traditions based on the ways of the Old Norse. Getting together for occasional sumbels is a great way to commune with like-minded people. How your sumbel will look is only limited by your imagination. It might be set up and fancy, like a holiday dinner, with six or eight people sitting around a nicely laid out dining room table, passing around a drinking horn, or glass of mead, where each in turn praises and gives thanks to the gods for all they have received.

It could also be more like a neighborhood barbeque. Folding chairs, set in a circle, under a shade tree. The specifics of the setting and food are up to you. Be sure though that if you are calling it a sumbel you treat it as such. Someone, you, or an assigned person, should be in charge of keeping the conversation on task. The hávamál cautions, "Shun not the mead, but drink in measure; Speak to the point or be still" [108].

In other words, enjoy the alcohol, you would not be honoring Odin without it, but do not get sloppy drunk, that does not honor anyone. Also, stay focused on why you have come together. Keep the conversation relevant and to the point. You may want to hang out and get to know each other, but during the Sumbel it is not appropriate. Once the gods have been given their due, by pouring out the wine or mead onto the earth, and the Sumbel has been concluded, then it would be a great time to get to know each other, share a communal meal and enjoy the fellowship of other heathens and Norse Pagans.

Decide ahead of time whether you will have a hlautbowl (an honoring bowl) to pour any remaining alcohol into once it has made its round among those present. If you do not have something to use as an honoring bowl, then the person who gave the toast will pour that portion onto the ground for the gods and land wights to enjoy. If the sumbel is taking place indoors, using a hlautbowl allows the ceremony to move along more smoothly. It would not be appropriate to just grab an old bowl or pitcher from your cupboard to use. It should be something dedicated to that purpose. If you do not have one, perhaps someone else in the group does. This is a group event after all.

You do not need a formal ceremony, like a sumbel, to get together with other heathens. Get together for a cup of coffee, get to know each other, and discuss different aspects of Norse paganism or what traits of the Vikings you are working towards emulating. It is human nature to want to share, and brag about our accomplishments. You may have been raised that it is wrong to brag or speak highly of yourself. Norse pagans enjoy talking about all the things they have achieved or are working towards. It is part of the lifestyle, but there is proper etiquette to be observed. Brag up to and including your best recent accomplishment, but do not inflate the truth. Telling the truth and speaking honestly is one of the strongest principles the Old Norse lived by. In the hávamál it says. "Happy the one who wins for himself favor and praises fair" [108].

The hávamál also warns against getting too big of a head. "A man shall not boast of his keenness of mind but keep it close in his breast" It is all about keeping things in balance. The desire for approval starts in infancy and does not stop until our life is over. "Happy the man who has while he lives wisdom and praise as well." Talk about your actual achievements, instead of bragging about how smart you are [108].

Every religion has its own mythology on which it is based. That statement might be controversial, but it is true. What is considered "fact" by the believers of any religion is a myth or story to people outside that religious tradition.

The song, "From a Distance," discusses what is happening on earth, from space, from a vantage point of distance [111].

When we step back and view things from a broader perspective, beyond ego and dogma, and the weight of family traditions that go back generations, we are able to look at Christianity and Norse Paganism, side by side as equals. Then you can decide for yourself which set of beliefs better fits your goals and desires, the way you think, and your dreams for yourself in the future.

Conclusion

At the beginning of this book, I made you, the reader, a promise. I hope you feel that I've accomplished that. Over the past several years there have been a plethora of new books about Norse Paganism on the market. I have bought the majority of them and finished most. With some, I will not name names, it was obvious that the writer had no genuine understanding of what they were writing about. So, I decided to write a book myself. I am not a scholar of paganism or Norse rituals. I am a self-taught heathen, a Norse pagan with deep admiration and respect for the Norse pantheon of gods. I am grateful for the strengths and values I have gained because of my pagan beliefs.

There were times while putting down my thoughts for this book, that I could feel the goddess Freyja. Her breath on my shoulder, her voice a whisper in my ear. She pushed me to step outside of my comfort zone. It was her I felt at those times when I thought of backing off and not dedicating a chapter to the issues created by the misrepresentation of *Germania*. Racism is not a comfortable topic to discuss, but to avoid it would be cowardly. Being bold and brave are just two of the traits that have grown within me since becoming a Norse pagan. The Norse gods and goddesses are tough. How could I count myself worthy of their guidance if I was not brave enough to confront the anvil of White Supremacy that for too long has hung over Norse pagan beliefs?

I felt my ancestors, especially my maternal grandmother, with me as well. She is the one that introduced me to all the land wights that lived in the rustic fairy garden behind her house. I was not allowed to walk in it. It was their home and I needed to respect that boundary. She taught me how to leave them food or a gift of beads and little trinkets that could be used to decorated the landscape of the spirits' homes, a moss-covered ground with wild mushrooms popping up here and there. Multiple birds made nests in the branches of the trees above it all. When the sun was just right, little flashes of reflected light would pop off the bird's nests, and I could see where a stolen trinket from below had been swooped up and was sticking out from between the twigs and leaves of the nest.

If you are already a Norse Pagan, I hope reading this book has ignited a deeper love and commitment to your beliefs, and that it has given you ideas on how to integrate those pagan beliefs into your life on a more regular basis. For those not already heathen, I hope this book opens your mind to the positive role Norse Paganism can have in your life. I did not write this book as a textbook on Norse Pagan beliefs. If you are new to Norse Paganism, I encourage you to learn more. Discover Yggdrasil, the World Tree, and the intricate and complex universe that exists within its branches. Learn about the fascinating worlds of giants and elves. Discover how talented the dwarfs truly are. Perhaps that will be my next project.

I encourage you to reach out and meet other Norse pagans. In discussing runes, I invited you to visit my webpage and download directions on how to make your own. Please do, and while you are there, take a look around. It is in its early infancy, but my hope is that with your help and input it will grow into a hub where Norse Pagans get to know each other and share stories about their own pagan journey. There is a place to post upcoming events, that you know about or are in your area, that might be of interest to others. For example, most years there is a multi-day Viking Festival that sets up about an hour's drive from where I live. Due to Covid, they couldn't set up last year, but we have our fingers crossed for 2022. For those interested in "pagans in the news" or who want to discuss different issues that affect our community there is a place for that as well. No hate, politics, or non-pagan topics.

When I finish here this evening and set my pen down. I will light the candles on my altar, give thanks to the gods and goddesses for their help in my journey to write this book. Then I will share my wine with them, the land-wights outside, my ancestors, and I will raise a toast to you.

If you enjoyed this book, please consider leaving a review, it would be greatly appreciated.

References

[1] DeSimone, D. (2021, February 10). What are the Mottos of the 6 Branches of the U.S. Military? United Service Organizations. https://www.uso.org/stories/2990-what-are-the-mottos-of-the-6-branches-of-the-u-s-military

[2] Levine, A. (2012, November 12). Popular US Army Slogans, Sayings, and Mottos. Custom Ink. https://blog.customink.com/2012/11/army-slogans-sayings/

[3] Oct 22, 2018 by Brandon Gaille 50 Best Marine Slogans and Mottos. https://brandongaille.com/50-best-marine-corps-slogans-and-mottos-ever/

[4] Veteran Car Donations. (2021, May 10). U.S. Military

Mottos and Their Meanings. https://www.veterancardonations.org/blog/us-military-mottos-and-what-they-mean/

[5] The British Army. (Accessed 10/14/2021) The Royal Gurkha Rifles https://www.army.mod.uk/who-we-are/corps-regiments-and-units/brigade-of-gurkhas/the-royal-gurkha-rifles/

[6] ShortHistory.com (Accessed 10/14/2021) Who Were the Varangians? https://www.shorthistory.org/middle-ages/who-were-the-varangians/

[7] MilitaryHistory.Fandom.com (Accessed 10/17/2021) List of Military Units Mottos by Country https://military-history.fandom.com/wiki/List_of_military_unit_mottoes_by_country

[8] Tacitus, C. translators A.J. Church and W.J. Brodribb. Germania. 1877 https://sourcebooks.fordham.edu/source/tacitus1.asp

[9] IMDb. All Viking/Norse Movies and TV Shows. 12/19/2016. https://www.imdb.com/list/ls066440877/?ref_=otl_1

[10] IMDb. The Viking. https://www.imdb.com/title/tt0019532/

[11] A-Z List of Marvel Comic Characters | Marvel Comic Characters List. (n.d.). Marvel Entertainment. https://www.marvel.com/comics/characters

[12] Wikipedia contributors. (2022, February 9). Norse mythology in popular culture. Wikipedia. https://en.wikipedia.org/wiki/Norse_mythology_in_popular_culture

[13] Rouă, V. (2021, June 4). 10 Influences From The Norse Mythology In J.R.R. Tolkien's Works. The Dockyards. https://www.thedockyards.com/10-facts-j-r-r-tolkien-influenced-norse-culture/

[14] Grammaticus, Saxo. H.E. Davidson Ed., Fisher, P. Trans. Saxo Grammaticus: The History of the Danes Book I-IX (first published approx. 1187) BOYE6. 2008.

[15] IMDb Viking Movies https://www.imdb.com/find?q=vikings&s=tt&ttype=ft&ref_=fn_ft

[16] IMDb.com The Viking (1928) https://www.imdb.com/title/tt0019532/

[17] Wigington, Patty. (July 5, 2019) LearnReligions.com *Asatru - Norse Heathens of Modern Paganism*

https://www.learnreligions.com/asatru-modern-paganism-2562545

[18] Schoppert, S. (2021, October 8). *Centuries of Fear: 6 Superstitions from the Middle Ages.* HistoryCollection.Com. https://historycollection.com/centuries-fear-superstitions-middle-ages/

[19] *Snorri Sturluson: His Life and Work.* (n.d.). Vsnrweb Publications. http://www.vsnrweb-publications.org.uk/Snorri%20Sturluson%20(Viking%20World).pdf

[20] Sturluson, S. The Prose Edda. Penguin Classics, 2006

[21] Guide to Iceland and https://octavia.net/arni-magnusson-institute/

[22] Bellows, H.A. (translator) *The Poetic Edda the Heroic Poems.* Dover Publications. 1936 reprinted 1997

[23] Crawford, J. *The Poetic Edda: Stories of the Norse Gods and Heroes.* Hackett Publishing Company, Inc., Indianapolis. 2015

[24] Bugge, A. (1909). The Origin and Credibility of the Icelandic Saga. *The American Historical Review,* 14(2), 249–261. https://doi.org/10.2307/1832657

[25] Crawford, J. *The Saga of the Volsungs with the Saga of Ragnar Lothbrik.* Hackett Publishing Company, Inc., Indianapolis. 2017

[26] Oxford University Press. (2014, August 25). Who was Saxo Grammaticus? OUPblog. https://blog.oup.com/2014/09/who-was-saxo-grammaticus/

[27] Vučković, A. Saxo Grammaticus: Warrior Historian of the Danes and a Medieval Influencer. April 14,2021 Ancient-Origins.net https://www.ancient-origins.net/history-famous-people/saxo-grammaticus-0015194

[28] Tacitus | Roman historian. (2022, January 1). Encyclopedia Britannica. https://www.britannica.com/biography/Tacitus-Roman-historian

[29] History of Germania. Germania Mint. https://germaniamint.com/history-of-germania/

[30] Simon, E. T. (2008, February 21). *Ancient text has long and dangerous reach: Tacitus helped fuel Nazi propaganda with 'Germania.'* Harvard Gazette. https://news.harvard.edu/gazette/story/2008/02/ancient-text-has-long-and-dangerous-reach/

[31] Atlantic, T. (2018, August 25). What To Do When

Racists Try To Hijack Your Religion. Medium. https://medium.com/the-atlantic/what-to-do-when-racists-try-to-hijack-your-religion-a676904baed0

[32] Darensburg, W. B. Y. J. (2017, March 25). Norse mythology and the Nazis. JD's Blog-o-Rama. https://jasondarensburg.wordpress.com/2015/07/10/norse-mythology-and-the-nazis/

[33] Tacitus, C. translator Gordon, T. by *Germania.* 1910 https://www.gutenberg.org/files/2995/2995-h/2995-h.htm"

[34] Tacitus, C. translators A.J. Church and W.J. Brodribb. Germania. 1877 https://sourcebooks.fordham.edu/source/tacitus1.asp

[35] Color image of Adolf Hitler's face. https://rarehistoricalphotos.com/rare-color-photo-adolf-hitler-shows-true-eye-color-date-unknown/

[36] Dean, M. *How Tall was Hitler?* Facts/People June 20,2020 http://www.worldwar2facts.org/how-tall-was-hitler.html

[37] C N Trueman "Ancient Rome and Trade" historylearningsite.co.uk. The History Learning Site, 16 Mar 2015. 2 Jan 2022.

[38] Department of Ancient Near Eastern Art. "Trade between Arabia and the Empires of Rome and Asia." In *Heilbrunn Timeline of Art History*. New York: The Metropolitan Museum of Art, 2000–. http://www.metmuseum.org/toah/hd/ince/hd_ince.htm (October 2000)

[39] Cock-Starkey, C. 8 Trade Routes That Shaped World History. https://www.mentalfloss.com/article/86338/8-trade-routes-shaped-world-history Sept 20,2016 (Updated June 4, 2020)

[40] Johnson, B. Timeline of Roman Britain. Historic UK: The History and Heritage Accommodation Guide. 22nd January 2015 https://www.historic-uk.com/HistoryUK/HistoryofBritain/Timeline-of-Roman-Britain

[41] Hopkins, K. Christian Number and its Implications. Oct 20,2017 Cambridge University Press. https://www.cambridge.org/core/books/abs/sociological-studies-in-roman-history/christian-number-and-its-implications/0AF33DAAA8313EB9BF282ED3AD5E64F9

[42] Gibbons, A. Science.org. There's no such thing as a 'pure' European—or anyone else: Most of us are a mishmash of many migrations over thousands of years. 15 May 2017.

https://www.science.org/content/article/theres-no-such-thing-pure-european-or-anyone-else

[43] Hay, M. The Genetic causes ethnic origins and history of red hair Eupedia.com accessed 14/1/2022 https://www.eupedia.com/genetics/origins_of_red_hair.shtml

[44] Anderson, R. Prose Edda Introduction 1979

[45] Dawe, L.S. Names and Epithets of Odin. Wytch of the North. July 19, 2015 https://wytchofthenorth.wordpress.com/2015/07/19/30-days-of-odin-day-7/

[46] Christensen, C. (2021, November 19). This is Why Odin Sacrificed His Eye in Norse Mythology. Scandinavia Facts. https://scandinaviafacts.com/this-is-why-odin-sacrificed-his-eye/

[47] Greenberg, M., PhD. (2021, June 24). Hugin and Munin: A Complete Guide to the Ravens of the Mind. Mythology Source. https://mythologysource.com/hugin-munin-odin-ravens/

[48] Ymir. (2018, September 4). Norse Mythology for Smart People. https://norse-mythology.org/gods-and-creatures/giants/ymir/

[49] Thor. (2019, February 9). Norse Mythology for Smart People. https://norse-mythology.org/gods-and-creatures/the-aesir-gods-and-goddesses/thor/

[50] Thor the Transvestite. (2017, July 9). Norse Mythology for Smart People. https://norse-mythology.org/tales/thor-the-transvestite/

[51] Elly. (2018, December 1). Lesson from Mjolnir Hammer of Thor in Norse Myth. BaviPower. https://bavipower.-com/blogs/bavipower-viking-blog/lesson-from-mjolnir-hammer-of-thor-in-norse-myth.

[52] Short, W. The Treasures of the Gods. Hurstwic LLC http://www.hurstwic.org/history/articles/mythology/myths/text/treasures

[53] Sturluson, S. The Prose Edda, Skáldskaparmál

[54] *Thor's Shrine: Who is Thor?* (n.d.). Northern Paganism. https://www.northernpaganism.org/shrines/thor/who-is-thor.html

[55] American's Got Talent. (2021, June 8). Golden Buzzer: Nightbirde's Original Song Makes Simon Cowell Emotional – America's Got Talent 2021. https://www.youtube.com/watch?v=CZJvBfoHDko&t=317s

[56] Gaille, B. (2017, May 30). 17 Profound Transgender Hate Crime Statistics. BrandonGaille. https://brandongaille.com/15-profound-transgender-hate-crime-statistics/

[57] Quinlan, C. (2021, Sept. 1). Anti-transgender hate crimes rose dramatically in 2020. The American Independent. https://americanindependent.com/anti-transgender-lgbtq-hate-crimes-fbi-report-2020

[58] Story, J. (n.d.). *The Viking Attack on Lindisfarne.* EnglishHeritage.org. https://www.english-heritage.org.uk/visit/places/lindisfarne-priory/History/viking-raid

[59] Viking Archaeology. (n.d.). *A Timeline of Viking Raids.* http://viking.archeurope.com/raids/

[60] Nikel, D. (2020, December 3). *Viking Religion: From the Norse Gods to Christianity.* Life in Norway. https://www.lifeinnorway.net/viking-religion/

[61] Rodgers, D.G. (2019, March 26). *Vikings and Christianity.* Sons of Vikings. https://sonsofvikings.com/blogs/history/the-vikings-and-christianity

[62] Norse Mythology for Smart People. (2019, February 9). *The Vikings' Conversion to Christianity.* https://norse-mythology.org/the-vikings-conversion-to-christianity/

[63] Viking.No. (2015, June 22). *The Vikings meet Christianity*. https://www.viking.no/who-were-the-vikings/the-vikings-meet-christianity/

[64] Shea, C. (2011, June 6). *The effects of Germanic mythology on Christianity and the creation of a Germanic Christianity*: an honors thesis (HONRS 499). Cardinal Scholar. https://cardinalscholar.bsu.edu/handle/handle/189970

[65] Medieval Chronicles. (2020, August 14). Medieval Witchcraft And Wicked Witches! https://www.medievalchronicles.com/medieval-torture-devices/medieval-witchcraft/

[66] Shakespeare, W. Shakespeare Select Plays Macbeth. Claredon Press. Oxford. 1871. https://www.google.com/books/edition/Macbeth/2WJ9x_PVVOQC?hl=en&gbpv=1&printsec=frontcover

[67] The Disney Wiki. (n.d.). *The Sorcerer's Apprentice*. https://disney.fandom.com/wiki/The_Sorcerer%27s_Apprentice

[68] Medievalists.net. (2020, June 28). *Farming with Charms in the Middle Ages*. https://www.medievalists.net/2020/06/farming-with-charms-in-the-middle-ages/

[69] Medievalists.net. (2021, September 6). *Everyday Magic in the Middle Ages*. https://www.medievalists.net/2021/09/everyday-magic-middle-ages/

[70] Hostetter, Dr. A.K. (n.d.) *The Metrical Charms I: For Unfruitful Land*. Camdin. https://oldenglishpoetry.camden.rutgers.edu/the-metrical-charms/

[71] Norse Mythology for Smart People. (2018, July 10). *Magic*. https://norse-mythology.org/concepts/magic/

[72] Tacitus, C. translator Gordon, T. by *Germania*. 1910 https://www.gutenberg.org/files/2995/2995-h/2995-h.htm"

[73] Skjalden. (2021, April 15). *Völva the Viking Witch or Seeress*. Nordic Culture. https://skjalden.com/volva-the-viking-witch-or-seeress/

[74] Flowers, S. The Galdrabók An Icelandic Grimoire. Samuel Weiser, Inc. York Beach. 1989 https://www.academia.edu/35888089/Galdrabok_an_icelandic_grimoire_1_?email_work_card=view-paper

[75] McCoy, D. (2016). The Viking Spirit.

[76] Norse Mythology for Smart People. (2018, July 9).

Shamanism. https://norse-mythology.org/concepts/shamanism/

[77] Geller. (2018, July 7). *Berserker.* Mythology.Net. https://mythology.net/norse/norse-creatures/berserker/

[78] Groeneveld, E. (2022, February 19). *Runes.* World History Encyclopedia. https://www.worldhistory.org/runes/

[79] World-Tree Project. (n.d.). *Runes of divination and magic? · Misconceptions and Misunderstandings.* World Tree Project. http://www.worldtreeproject.org/exhibits/show/miscon/magrun

[80] Sigrdriftfumol the Ballad of The Victory-Bringer (accessed 8/27/21). https://www.sacred-texts.com/neu/poe/poe25.htm

[81] Croarkin, S. (2010). *The Effects of Germanic Mythology on Christianity and the Creation of a Germanic Christianity.* Master's Thesis. Ball State University. https://cardinalschol-ar.bsu.edu/handle/handle/189970

[82] National Museum of Denmark. (n.d.). The Viking blót sacrifices. Prehistoric period/ The Viking Age, Religion, Magic, Death, and Rituals. https://en.natmus.dk/historical-knowledge/denmark/prehistoric-period-until-1050-ad/the-

viking-age/religion-magic-death-and-rituals/the-viking-blot-sacrifices/

[83] Simek, R.(1996). *Blót à Sacrifice*. The Dictionary of Northern Mythology. Boydell & Brewer Ltd. Suffolk UK.

[84] Kammerud, Clements, Musker, Smith, Holmes (Directors). (1989). Little Mermaid. The Walt Disney Company.

[85] Groeneveld, E. (2018, Aug. 31). *Ragnar Lothbrok*. WorldHistory.org. https://www.worldhistory.org/Ragnar_Lothbrok

[86] Riseley, C. (2014). Ceremonial Drinking in the Viking Age. University of Oslo, Dept. of Viking and Medieval Norse studies. https://core.ac.uk/download/pdf/30902714.pdf

[87] Sturluson, S. The Prose Edda. Penguin Classics, 2006

[88] Hallakarva, G. (1991 Issue 2 Autumn). *Basics of Sumbel*. Mountain Thunder. http://www.thewhitegoddess.co.uk/articles/general_pagan/basics_of_sumbel.asp

[89] Gomes, M. (2011, March 27). Symbel / Bragafull. https://marcelgomessweden.wordpress.com/2011/03/27/symbel-bragafull/

[90] History with Hilbert. (n.d. accessed 3/28/22) YouTube video The Pagan Roots of Christmas. https://www.youtube.-com/watch?v=LliqvacoNu8

[91] Totenberg, M. (2020, Dec. 9) Digging up the roots of holiday traditions: Christmas. Tenement Museum. https://www.tenement.org/blog/digging-up-the-roots-of-holiday-traditions-christmas/

[92] Scandinavian Christmas traditions. (n.d.) *Old Norse Yule.* https://www.scandinavianchristmastraditions.com/oldnorseyule.html

[93] Lipzinski, A. (2018, Dec 7). Where Does the Tradition of Gift-Giving Come From Anyway? The Lode. https://mtulode.com/2739/pulse/where-does-the-tradition-of-gift-giving-come-from-anyway/

[94] Mueller, N. (2017, Dec. 16). Evergreen trees for the darkest days: The ancient roots of Christmas trees. Society of Ethnobiology. https://ethnobiology.org/forage/blog/ever-greens-darkest-days-ancient-roots-christmas-trees

[95] Kaldera, R. (2014). *Ostara: Who is Ostara?* NorthernPa-ganism.org. https://www.northernpaganism.org/shrines/ostara/about.html

[96] Sargent, R. (2020, Dec.21). Pagan Holidays That Have Made Their Way Into Everyday Christianity. Ranker. https://www.ranker.com/list/christian-holidays-with-pagan-origins/ryan-sargent

[97] Siegfried, Dr. K.E.H. (2015, Dec. 29). Norse Mythology's Endless Appeal. The Norse Mythology Blog. https://www.norsemyth.org/2015/12/norse-mythologys-endless-appeal.html

[98] Seven Trees Farm. (2013, Feb. 3). *Charming of the Plow*. https://seventreesfarm.wordpress.com/2013/02/03/charming-of-the-plow/

[99] McCoy, D. (2016). The Viking Spirit.

[100] Viking Chamber of Commerce. (n.d.) Top 8 Viking Norse Germanic Holidays. http://vikingchamber.org/top-8-viking-norse-germanic-holidays

[101] 5y1.org. (n.d.). Ostara Rituals and Traditions. https://5y1.org/info/ostara-rituals-and-traditions_2_b3bb4b.html

[102] Valkyrja. (2017, April 20) The Four Main blots of the blóts of the year. http://valkyrja.com/200417.html

[103] Pederson. J.P. (2013, July 7). Midsummer. Heidnibok

Norseman's Codex of Heathenism. http://heidnibok. blogspot.com/search?q=Midsummer%E2%80%99s+Day

[104] Fornkunskap. (2014, Oct. 1) Vetrnætr. https://fornkun-skap.wordpress.com/2014/10/01/vetrnaetr/

[105] Winternights Festival. (n.d.) *About Vetrnaetr.* https:// winternightsfestival.com/about-vetrnaetr/

[106] Sites used for Bible verses: Bible.org , Biblereasons.com , Biblestudytools.com , Christianity.com , Concordia.edu , Dailyverses.net , Embracingsimplerlife.com , Kingjamesbibleonline.org , openbible.info

[107] Tacitus, C. translator Gordon, T. by *Germania.* 1910 https://www.gutenberg.org/files/2995/2995-h/2995-h.htm"

[108] Bellows, H.A. (translator) *Hávamál, The Poetic Edda the Heroic Poems.* Dover Publications. 1936 reprinted 1997

[109] Wikipedia. (n.d.) Ignorance. https://en.wikipedia.org/ wiki/Ignorance

[110] S. Eric. (2012) Heimdall Bifrost's Guardian. NorsePa-ganism.org. https://norsepaganism.org/ shrines/Heimdall.html

[111] Gold, J. (1985). From a Distance [Recorded by Bette Midler 1990]. On Some People's Lives Album.

Other Resources:

Crawford, J. *The Saga of the Volsungs with the Saga of Ragnar Lothbrik*. Hackett Publishing Company, Inc., Indianapolis. 2017

Crawford, J. *The Poetic Edda: Stories of the Norse Gods and Heroes*. Hackett Publishing Company, Inc., Indianapolis. 2015

Davidson, H.R. *Myths and Symbols in Pagan Europe: Early Scandinavian and Celtic Religions*. Syracuse University Press. Syracuse. 1988

Department of the Army. (1982) *Jungle Operations* (FM 90-5). https://irp.fas.org/doddir/army/fm90-5.pdf

Dougherty, M.J. *Vikings a History of the Norse People*. Amber Books. 2016

Lafayllve, P.M. *The Practical Heathen's Guide to Asatru*. Llewellyn Publications. Woodbury. 2013.

Larrington, C. *The Norse Myths: A Guide to the Gods and Heroes.* Thames & Hudson Ltd. London. 2021

Miller, W.I. *Bloodtaking and Peacemaking: Feud, Law, and Society in Saga Iceland.* The University of Chicago Press. Chicago. 1996

Peschel, Lisa. A Practical Guide to the Runes. Llewellyn's New Age Series. 2001

Saemundr the Learned. *The Poetic Edda.* Corundum Classics (1st Pub. 13th century CE)

Simek, R. *Dictionary of Northern Mythology.* Cambridge. 1996.

Sturluson, S. The Prose Edda. Penguin Classics, 2006

A special note

If you are interested in a great source for all of the Icelandic Sagas, I don't know of one better than Icelandic Saga Database: https://sagadb.org/

It is a non-profit organization. I would encourage anyone that enjoys the Sagas and wants to help make sure they continue to be accessible to all, to support their work. I have no affiliation with them but I am sure they could use any and all donations they receive.

If you would like a free copy of my eBook, "How to Create Your Own Futhark Runes"

Visit our website at Modernheathenspress.com

While you are there, look around. The site is in its infancy, but we will be adding more to it all the time.

You will also find interesting Norse Pagan information, like the complete list of Odin's names.

There are also links to free online English versions of various Old Norse text such as Prose Edda.